GRAND JUNCTION

HIKING GUIDE
2025

EXPLORING RUGGED TRAILS AND HIDDEN PEAKS

BRIAN M. TAYLOR

Disclaimer

The world is constantly changing, hotels change ownership or close, restaurants might adjust their prices, museum could alter their closing hours, and transportation routes can be modified.

This changes can happen even after our author have visited, inspected and written about these places

While we strive to keep all information as current as possible, some changes may inevitable occur before a new edition of this guidebook is published.

Thanks you for choosing our guidebook, we hope you have an amazing trip

About the Author

Hiking has always been more than just a passion for me—it's a way of life. From the towering peaks of the Rockies to the rugged deserts of the American Southwest, I've spent years exploring the most breathtaking landscapes nature has to offer. My journey as a travel and hiking guidebook author began with a simple goal: to create guides that don't just list trails, but truly prepare and inspire hikers for unforgettable adventures.

Grand Junction holds a special place in my heart. Its dramatic canyons, hidden waterfalls, and stunning high-desert terrain make it one of the most diverse and underrated hiking destinations in the country. In this guide, I've poured my firsthand experiences, insider tips, and storytelling into every page—ensuring you don't just see Grand Junction, but truly experience it.

Through this book, I hope to take the guesswork out of planning your trip, helping you find the best trails, avoid common mistakes, and make the most of your time in this incredible landscape. Whether you're a first-time hiker or an experienced backpacker, I want this guide to be your trusted companion on the trail.

Happy hiking—see you out there!

1. "The most detailed and well-organized hiking guide I've ever used!"

"As an avid hiker, I've relied on countless guidebooks, but this one truly stands out. The descriptions are spot-on, the insights are invaluable, and the storytelling makes you feel like you're already on the trail. Whether you're looking for an easy scenic stroll or a grueling backcountry trek, this guide has it all!"

— *Mark T., Colorado Outdoor Enthusiast*

2. "A must-have for any hiker visiting Grand Junction!"

"This guide saved me so much time planning my trip. It not only covers the best trails but also gives real, practical advice on weather, gear, and avoiding common mistakes. Thanks to this book, I had an unforgettable experience hiking in Grand Junction!"

— *Lisa R., Weekend Explorer*

3. "Perfect for both beginners and experienced hikers!"

"I was new to hiking, and this guide helped me choose the right trails without feeling overwhelmed. The difficulty ratings, safety tips, and recommendations were incredibly useful. My more experienced hiking friends also loved the challenging trail suggestions!"

— *Jessica W., First-Time Hiker*

4. "The ultimate trail companion—accurate, engaging, and packed with insider tips!"

"I've hiked in Grand Junction before, but this book showed me hidden gems I never knew existed! The trail descriptions are detailed and realistic, so there were no surprises. Plus, the Leave No Trace and safety tips were a great reminder for responsible hiking."

— David P., Seasoned Backpacker

5. "Way better than just Googling trails—this book gives real, useful info!"

"I've been disappointed by online trail reviews before, but this guide was a game-changer. It tells you exactly what to expect, from terrain and weather to the best times to visit. I felt fully prepared for my hikes and even discovered some of the best post-hike breweries thanks to the bonus section!"

— Michelle L., Adventure Traveler

Gratitude

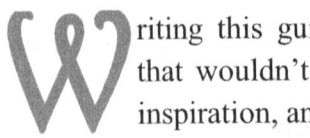riting this guide has been an incredible journey—one that wouldn't have been possible without the support, inspiration, and encouragement of so many people.

First, to the local hikers, park rangers, and outdoor enthusiasts who generously shared their insights—your knowledge and passion for Grand Junction's trails made this book richer and more authentic. Thank you for your wisdom, stories, and advice.

To my family and friends, who have always believed in my work, even when I disappeared for long days in the wilderness—your patience and encouragement mean the world to me.

To the readers—whether you're a first-time hiker or a seasoned explorer—thank you for trusting this guide. My hope is that it helps you experience Grand Junction in the most rewarding way possible.

Finally, to the trails themselves—every step taken, every view earned, and every challenge faced has been a lesson. Here's to many more adventures ahead!

Warm Regard

Brian M. Taylor

This Guide Book Belong To

_____

_____

_____

Introduction **11**

Why Grand Junction? What Makes It a Unique Hiking Destination... 13

How to Use This Guide: Finding the Right Hike for You 15

Hiking Responsibly: Leave No Trace & Trail Etiquette 16

What to Expect: Terrain, Climate & Seasonal Changes..................... 19

Common Myths & Misconceptions About Hiking in Grand Junction. 22

Planning Your Trip **25**

Best Time to Visit: Month-by-Month Guide..................................... 26

Getting There: Flights, Road Trips & Local Transportation 29

Where to Stay: Hiker-Friendly Hotels, Campgrounds & RV Parks...... 31

Packing Smart: Essential Gear, Clothing & Safety Items 33

Finding The Perfect Trail: What You Need To Know **39**

Types of Trails in Grand Junction... 40

How Trails Are Rated: Understanding Easy, Moderate & Difficult
Ratings 41

Altitude & Acclimatization: How to Avoid Altitude Sickness............. 44

Best Trails by Type:... 45

Wildlife & Plants: What You Might Encounter on the Trails 50

Hiking with Kids & Dogs: Trails That Are Safe & Fun for Everyone 52

Best Hikes In Grand Junction **56**

EASY & FAMILY-FRIENDLY TRAILS... 57

Dinosaur Hill Trail – A Walk Through Prehistoric History................... 58

Riverfront Trail – Relaxing Views Along the Colorado River 59

Miramonte Rim Trail – Easy Trail with Panoramic Views................... 60

Liberty Cap Trail (Lower Section) – A Beginner-Friendly Rock Climb. 61

MODERATE TRAILS (For Adventurous Hikers) **63**

Serpents Trail – The "Crookedest Road" Now a Stunning Hike 64

No Thoroughfare Canyon – Hidden Waterfalls & Stunning Rock Walls 65

Mica Mine Trail – A Trail with Glittering Rocks & Mining History 67

Liberty Cap Trail (Full Route) – A Tougher Climb with Great Rewards 68

Echo Canyon Trail – A Trail with Pools, Waterfalls & Red Rock Walls 70

CHALLENGING TRAILS (For Experienced Hikers) **72**

Ute Canyon Trail – A True Wilderness Experience 74

Rattlesnake Arches Trail – Second Largest Arch Collection in the World 76

Palisade Plunge – One of Grand Junction's Longest & Most Epic Trails 77

Fruita Paleo Area to Pollock Bench – A Rugged, Remote Trek 79

Multi-Day Hikes & Backpacking Adventures **81**

Hidden Gems: Underrated Trails That Are Worth Exploring 82

Best Routes for a Weekend Adventure (For Those Looking for Overnight Hikes) 83

Camping on the Trail: Where to Set Up Camp & What to Pack 85

GRAND JUNCTION HIKING ITINERARIES **88**

24 Hours in Grand Junction: The Best Quick Hikes 89

3-Day Ultimate Hiking & Sightseeing Plan (Includes Food & Rest Stop Suggestions) 91

One Week in Grand Junction: A Hiker's Dream Schedule 93

SEASONAL HIKING IN GRAND JUNCTION **96**

Spring: Best Wildflower Trails & Waterfall Hikes 97

Summer: Beating the Heat & Staying Hydrated on the Trail 99

Fall: Best Trails for Colorful Foliage & Cooler Temperatures 102

Winter: Snowy Trails, Ice Hiking & Cold-Weather Safety Tips 104

Beyond Hiking: Other Adventures In Grand Junction **107**

Best Rock Climbing & Bouldering Spots 108

Top Mountain Biking Trails in the Region.................................... 110

Rafting & Kayaking on the Colorado River 113

Best Local Breweries & Wineries for a Post-Hike Drink 116

Local Insights & Expert Tips **118**

Interviews with Local Hikers & Park Rangers 119

Expert Tips for Hiking in Grand Junction 122

Trail Safety: What to Do in Case of an Emergency **124**

How to Avoid the Biggest Mistakes Hikers Make in Grand Junction 128

Practical Resources & Final Thoughts **132**

Best Hiking Apps & GPS Tools for Navigating Grand Junction 133

Where to Rent or Buy Hiking Gear Locally 134

Emergency Contacts & First Aid Advice for Hikers 135

Conclusion **138**

Bonus Section: Frequently Asked Questions (FAQ) **140**

New Updates & Expectations in 2025 142

WELCOME
TO

GRAND
JUNCTION

Chapter

1

Introduction

Standing at the edge of Colorado's rugged wilderness, Grand Junction is a paradise for hikers. Towering red rock formations, winding canyon trails, and sweeping views of the Colorado River set the stage for an adventure unlike any other. Whether you're a seasoned trekker craving a backcountry challenge or a beginner looking for a scenic stroll, this guide will help you navigate the best trails, hidden gems, and everything in between.

I remember my first hike in Grand Junction like it was yesterday. The sun was just peeking over the sandstone cliffs, casting long golden shadows across the desert floor. The air was crisp, carrying the faint scent of  juniper and sagebrush. With every step, the landscape revealed something new—a secret alcove, a towering monolith, a glimpse of a bighorn sheep effortlessly scaling the rocks. Grand Junction isn't just a place; it's an experience, one that leaves you in awe of nature's raw beauty.

This guide is designed to be your ultimate hiking companion. It's more than just a list of trails—it's a roadmap to the best adventures this region has to offer. You'll find detailed trail descriptions, insider tips, seasonal recommendations, and even itineraries to make the most of your trip.

I'll help you choose hikes based on your experience level, weather conditions, and what kind of adventure you're craving.

But more than that, I want to help you hike smarter, safer, and more responsibly. From packing essentials to avoiding common mistakes, I've packed this guide with everything you need to hit the trails with confidence.

So lace up your boots, take a deep breath, and get ready—because Grand Junction is calling, and it's time to answer. Let's hit the trails!

Why Grand Junction? What Makes It a Unique Hiking Destination

If you've ever dreamed of hiking through landscapes that feel like they belong in a Wild West adventure film, Grand Junction is the place to be. Located on the western edge of Colorado, this hiker's paradise is home to dramatic red rock canyons, towering sandstone spires, lush river valleys, and hidden desert oases. But what truly sets Grand Junction apart?

1. A Diverse Hiking Landscape

Unlike many hiking destinations that offer just one kind of terrain, Grand Junction gives you a little bit of everything. You can start your morning hiking through Colorado National Monument, where sheer-walled canyons and massive rock formations tower over the desert floor. By afternoon, you could be trekking through lush forests in the Grand Mesa, the world's largest flat-top mountain, where cool alpine lakes dot the landscape.

And if you're craving something remote, the Dominguez-Escalante National Conservation Area offers stunning solitude among waterfalls and petroglyphs.

2. Fewer Crowds, More Adventure

Unlike Colorado's more famous hiking destinations like Rocky Mountain National Park or Aspen's Maroon Bells, Grand Junction remains a bit of a hidden gem.

That means less trail congestion, fewer parking headaches, and more moments of solitude with breathtaking views. Even on popular trails, you'll often find yourself alone with nature, making your hikes feel more personal and immersive.

3. Hiking Year-Round

Most mountain destinations are buried under snow for half the year, but Grand Junction's lower elevation and desert climate make hiking possible in all seasons. Spring brings wildflowers, summer offers early morning canyon treks, fall paints the landscape in gold and red, and even winter provides sunny, snow-dusted trails perfect for a peaceful escape.

4. Rich History & Geology

Hiking in Grand Junction isn't just about the views—it's a walk through time. You'll trek past ancient petroglyphs, explore trails once traveled by Native American tribes, and witness rock formations shaped over millions of years. Some trails even lead to fossilized dinosaur tracks, making this a dream destination for history buffs and adventure seekers alike.

Whether you're looking for short, scenic strolls or multi-day backcountry treks, Grand Junction delivers.

It's an adventurer's playground, a nature lover's retreat, and a place that stays with you long after you've left.

How to Use This Guide: Finding the Right Hike for You

Every hiker is different. Some are chasing challenging ascents, while others want relaxing walks with epic views. This guide is designed to help you find the perfect trail based on your experience, time constraints, and what kind of adventure you're looking for.

1. Choosing the Right Difficulty Level

Easy Hikes (Under 3 miles, little elevation gain) – Perfect for beginners, families, or those looking for a laid-back experience. **Examples**: Devil's Kitchen, Dinosaur Hill Trail, Riverfront Trail.

Moderate Hikes (3–6 miles, moderate elevation gain) – For those who want a little challenge without going too extreme. **Examples**: Mica Mine Trail, Liberty Cap, Echo Canyon Trail.

Challenging Hikes (6+ miles, strenuous elevation gain) – Best for experienced hikers looking for a serious adventure. **Examples**: Monument Canyon Trail, Ute Canyon Trail, Rattlesnake Arches.

2. Finding the Best Hikes for Your Schedule

Only have a few hours? Stick to short, scenic hikes like Serpents Trail or Miramonte Rim.

A full day to explore? Take on longer trails like Monument Canyon or No Thoroughfare Canyon.

Multi-day backpacking adventure? Head deep into Dominguez Canyon for remote, backcountry beauty.

3. Seasonal Considerations

Spring & Fall – Best for hiking in canyons and desert landscapes (perfect weather, fewer bugs).

Summer – Ideal for higher-elevation trails like Grand Mesa to escape the heat.

Winter – Great for snow-free desert hikes, but bring layers for chilly mornings.

This guide is structured to make trip planning easy, with each hike clearly labeled for difficulty, distance, elevation gain, and estimated time. So whether you're a weekend warrior, a casual nature lover, or a hardcore backpacker, you'll find exactly what you need to make the most of your Grand Junction adventure.

Hiking Responsibly: Leave No Trace & Trail Etiquette

Hiking in Grand Junction means stepping into some of the most fragile and beautiful landscapes in the American West. With great adventure comes great responsibility, and it's up to all of us to keep these trails pristine, safe, and accessible for future generations.

1. Follow the 7 Leave No Trace Principles

The Leave No Trace principles are the gold standard for responsible hiking. Here's how they apply to Grand Junction's unique environment:

Plan Ahead & Prepare – Know your trail, pack enough water, and be ready for changing weather.

Travel & Camp on Durable Surfaces – Stay on marked trails to protect fragile desert plants and cryptobiotic soil (a living crust that prevents erosion).

Dispose of Waste Properly – Pack out everything you bring, including food scraps and toilet paper.

Leave What You Find – Don't take rocks, fossils, or plants. Grand Junction's beauty is best preserved as it is.

Minimize Campfire Impact – Avoid fires in dry areas. Instead, use a camping stove if you're backpacking.

Respect Wildlife – Keep your distance from bighorn sheep, snakes, and other native creatures.

Be Considerate of Others – Yield to uphill hikers, keep noise levels down, and give everyone space to enjoy nature.

2. Trail Etiquette for a Better Experience

Hikers going uphill have the right-of-way.

Stay Single File: Avoid widening trails by walking in a single line, especially in narrow areas.

Dogs on Leash: Grand Junction is dog-friendly, but many trails require leashes to protect wildlife and other hikers.

No Speaker Music: Nature's sounds are part of the experience. If you have to listen to music, put on headphones.

Respect Trail Closures: If a sign says a trail is closed, there's a reason—usually to protect wildlife or prevent damage.

3. Protecting Grand Junction's Unique Environment

Unlike alpine forests, desert ecosystems take decades to recover from damage.

Avoid stepping on cryptobiotic soil—that black, crusty surface is alive and crucial for preventing erosion.

Stick to established trails to prevent the creation of unnecessary paths.

Never carve into rock formations or leave graffiti—these landscapes belong to everyone and should remain untouched.

Final Thought: Leave It Better Than You Found It

When you leave a trail, no one should be able to tell you were there. Pick up extra trash, educate fellow hikers, and respect nature as if it were your own backyard—because in a way, it is.

Grand Junction's trails are some of the most breathtaking, diverse, and rewarding in the country. Let's keep them that way for generations to come.

What to Expect: Terrain, Climate & Seasonal Changes

When it comes to hiking in Grand Junction, the terrain, climate, and seasonal changes play an integral role in shaping your adventure. Whether you're planning to hike in the hot desert sun, or you're drawn to the cool mountain trails, understanding what to expect will help you prepare for the diverse and ever-changing conditions.

1. Terrain: A Landscape of Contrasts

Grand Junction sits at the confluence of the Colorado and Gunnison Rivers, offering an incredible variety of terrain, ranging from desert landscapes to mountainous forests.

Desert Canyons & Rock Formations: Trails like Monument Canyon and Ute Canyon wind through vast, open desert, offering breathtaking views of sandstone spires and red rock formations. These canyons are often rugged and rocky, requiring a bit of scrambling on some paths. The terrain here is dry, with lots of exposed rock and loose soil. Some trails may feature switchbacks, while others follow riverbeds or cliff edges. Expect a desert-like landscape that can be hot and dry, but with a wide variety of wildlife, such as lizards, snakes, and birds of prey.

Mountain Trails & Forests: As you venture to higher elevations, particularly in areas like Grand Mesa or The Book Cliffs, the landscape changes. These trails are marked by dense pine forests, alpine meadows, and cool mountain lakes. Here, the trails can be rocky and steep, and may even be lined with wildflowers in summer, providing a refreshing contrast to the desert.

Expect to find more gradual climbs on well-maintained paths as you ascend, with occasional rockier terrain near the summit.

River Valleys & Canyons: Grand Junction's diverse landscape also includes several river valley trails. The Colorado Riverfront Trail, for instance, is a flat, easy trail that follows the river's edge, giving you great views of the water and surrounding cliffs. This terrain is smoother and often paved, making it perfect for a casual hike or an easy family outing.

2. Climate: The Hot Desert and Alpine Coolness

Grand Junction's climate is typical of the Western Colorado Desert, with hot summers, mild winters, and a mix of temperatures depending on your elevation.

Summer (June - August): Temperatures can soar into the 90s or higher in the lower desert areas, with the intense heat sometimes making midday hikes feel unbearable. In the high desert, you'll experience cooler evenings, but the heat during the day can be relentless. For the mountain trails, summer brings warm, pleasant temperatures in the 60s and 70s in the higher altitudes, which makes for ideal hiking conditions. Hydration is key during the summer months, as heat and dry conditions can lead to quick dehydration.

Fall (September - November): Fall is one of the best times to visit Grand Junction. Temperatures in the desert cool down to the 60s and 70s, while the mountain trails can dip into the 50s and 60s. Autumn foliage adds a beautiful dimension to your hikes, especially on the Grand Mesa where golden aspens are in full swing. The cooler weather makes this season ideal for hiking, as the drier air allows for comfortable long treks.

Winter (December - February): The desert terrain in Grand Junction remains relatively mild, with temperatures ranging from the 30s to 50s during the day. However, the high desert can get quite cold at night, and it's not unusual to experience occasional snow flurries. In contrast, the mountain areas like Grand Mesa can see substantial snowfall, often making some trails impassable. Winter hiking in the lower elevations is possible and typically peaceful, with fewer crowds on the trails.

Spring (March - May): Spring in Grand Junction is when everything comes to life. Temperatures begin to warm up, reaching into the 60s to 80s in the desert and 50s to 60s in the mountains. Springtime offers a beautiful landscape filled with wildflowers, and the desert blooms with vibrant colors. This season is also the best time for moderate-length hikes, as the temperatures are manageable, and the trails aren't as hot as during the summer.

3. Seasonal Changes & Trail Conditions

The seasonal changes also affect trail conditions. During the spring and fall, most trails are easily accessible, but summer months may see increased trail maintenance, especially in high traffic areas. You'll want to check trail reports during the winter months for snow conditions, especially in the Grand Mesa area, where snow can accumulate and make trails slippery or impassable.

Common Myths & Misconceptions About Hiking in Grand Junction

There are several myths and misconceptions about hiking in Grand Junction that could keep some hikers from experiencing the adventure of a lifetime. Below is a summary of the most prevalent ones:

Myth 1: The Trails Are Too Hard for Beginners

Many people assume that Grand Junction is only for experienced hikers due to its rugged terrain and challenging climbs, but that couldn't be further from the truth. While there are definitely some challenging backcountry trails, there are also plenty of beginner-friendly hikes that showcase the area's beauty. Shorter trails like Dinosaur Hill or the Riverfront Trail offer easy, scenic walks, perfect for families, beginner hikers, or those with less hiking experience. Grand Junction's diverse trails provide something for all levels, from leisurely strolls to extreme backcountry adventures.

Myth 2: It's Too Hot to Hike in the Summer

It's true that Grand Junction can get scorching hot in the summer months, but the higher-altitude trails, such as those on the Grand Mesa, offer cooler temps and an excellent escape from the heat. Even in the desert, early morning and late afternoon hikes are manageable, as temperatures drop dramatically in the evenings. Hydration and sun protection are key to a safe and enjoyable summer hike, but with a little planning, hiking in the summer can still be a fantastic experience.

Myth 3: Grand Junction Is Only for Desert Hikes

While the desert landscapes of Grand Junction are undoubtedly the area's most iconic feature, it's a common misconception that it's all there is. In fact, the Grand Mesa offers lush forests, alpine lakes, and a cooler climate perfect for those who prefer mountain terrain. So, if you're someone who's not keen on desert hiking, rest assured—there's a whole other side to Grand Junction that is just as breathtaking.

Myth 4: Grand Junction Is Too Remote for Hiking Amenities

Many believe that since Grand Junction is relatively small and remote, hiking amenities like restrooms, water stations, and trailhead facilities are lacking. While some more remote trails may not have these amenities, Grand Junction is actually well-equipped for hikers. The Colorado National Monument and other popular areas are well-maintained with ample parking, water sources, and restrooms. Additionally, Grand Junction is home to a range of local outdoor shops where you can grab last-minute gear and advice from seasoned locals.

Myth 5: The Trails Are Overcrowded

Grand Junction is far less crowded than the more well-known Colorado hiking destinations like Aspen or Rocky Mountain National Park. Despite its popularity, the region remains relatively undiscovered by the average tourist, especially in areas like Dominguez Canyon or Ute Canyon. Many of the most iconic trails are remote and can offer you a private hiking experience, free from the crowds that often plague other parts of the state.

By busting these common myths, it becomes clear that Grand Junction is a diverse, accessible, and rewarding hiking destination.

Whether you're looking for challenging hikes or casual strolls, you'll find trails suited to your needs in this stunning corner of Colorado.

Chapter

2

Planning Your Trip

When it comes to hiking in Grand Junction, planning your trip can be just as rewarding as the adventure itself. From selecting the best time to visit to choosing your mode of transportation and deciding where to stay, careful planning ensures that you can make the most of your experience. This section will guide you through everything you need to know to plan a smooth, enjoyable, and memorable trip.

Best Time to Visit: Month-by-Month Guide

Grand Junction's weather can vary dramatically throughout the year, and understanding the best time to visit is crucial for ensuring you have an enjoyable hiking experience. Here's a month-by-month breakdown to help you decide the best time for your hiking trip.

January - February (Winter):

Temperatures: Winter temperatures in Grand Junction tend to be mild, but snow can blanket the higher elevations of the Grand Mesa and Book Cliffs. Expect daytime temperatures to hover between 30°F and 50°F in the desert, with colder conditions at night.

Why Visit: Winter is a great time for those seeking solitude on the trails. While mountain trails may be snow-covered, desert trails like those in Colorado National Monument are accessible and less crowded.

What to Expect: Peaceful hikes in the desert or low-altitude mountain trails. Be sure to check snow conditions before heading into the mountains.

March - May (Spring):

Temperatures: Spring brings mild temperatures ranging from the 50s to 80s in the desert and 40s to 60s in the mountains. The landscape starts to bloom, with wildflowers dotting the desert and forests.

Why Visit: This is arguably one of the best times to visit Grand Junction for hiking. The pleasant temperatures, lack of intense summer heat, and fewer tourists make for an ideal time to enjoy the region's trails.

What to Expect: Wildflowers in bloom, clearer skies, and moderate trail conditions. It's a perfect time for moderate to difficult hikes in the desert and mountains.

June - August (Summer):

Temperatures: Summer temperatures can soar into the 90s or higher in the desert, while mountain areas may offer cooler conditions in the 60s and 70s. Nights tend to cool down significantly.

Why Visit: If you're looking for higher-altitude hiking, the summer months are perfect for trails on the Grand Mesa and Book Cliffs. Early mornings and late evenings are the best times to hike in the desert.

What to Expect: Hot weather in the desert with opportunities to hike in the mountains where temperatures are cooler.

Trailheads near rivers like the Colorado Riverfront Trail also offer pleasant conditions in the early mornings.

September - November (Fall):

Temperatures: Fall sees temperatures in the 60s to 80s in the desert, with mountain temperatures dropping into the 50s and 60s. This is a beautiful time of year, with changing fall foliage.

Why Visit: Fall is another excellent season for hiking. The weather is cooler, the trails are often less crowded than summer, and the vibrant fall colors add an extra layer of beauty to the landscape.

What to Expect: Perfect hiking conditions for both desert and mountain trails. The fall foliage, especially on the Grand Mesa, is stunning, and there are fewer crowds, making it ideal for longer hikes.

December (Winter):

Temperatures: December sees temperatures range from the 30s to 50s in the desert, with colder temperatures in the mountains. Snow may start to accumulate at higher altitudes.

Why Visit: For those who enjoy hiking in peaceful solitude, winter is a good time to explore the desert landscape. Higher altitudes can be challenging due to snow, but desert trails remain open.

What to Expect: Quiet hikes with potential snow on mountain trails. If you're after a more serene hiking experience, winter is a beautiful time to visit.

Getting There: Flights, Road Trips & Local Transportation

Getting to Grand Junction is relatively straightforward, with options to suit all travelers. Whether you're flying in, taking a scenic road trip, or relying on local transportation, you'll find a variety of ways to reach the area.

By Air:

Grand Junction Regional Airport (GJT) is the closest major airport, located just 15 minutes from downtown Grand Junction. It serves direct flights from major cities like Denver, Salt Lake City, and Dallas.

Airlines: Delta, American Airlines, and United Airlines all operate regular flights to and from Grand Junction, with daily flights from Denver International Airport (DEN) being the most frequent. Rental cars are available at the airport for easy access to your hiking destination.

Flight Alternatives: If you can't find a direct flight, Denver International Airport (DEN) is the closest major airport with more extensive flight options. From Denver, it's a 4-hour drive to Grand Junction.

By Car (Road Trips):

Driving from Denver: The drive from Denver to Grand Junction is approximately 250 miles and takes about 4 hours. The journey is scenic, with views of the Rocky Mountains, high desert, and river valleys along the way.

Scenic Drives: Consider taking the Colorado National Monument Scenic Drive, which is a stunning drive through red rock canyons. If you're coming from Utah, you can drive along Interstate 70, which connects Grand Junction to Moab and other western destinations.

Road Conditions: The roads are well-maintained, but if traveling in the winter, be mindful of possible snow and icy conditions, especially in the mountains.

By Train:

Amtrak offers train service to Grand Junction via the California Zephyr route, which runs between Chicago and Emeryville (**California**), with stops in major cities like Denver and Salt Lake City.

The train station in Grand Junction is located in the downtown area, making it convenient for those who want to explore the city or head straight to their trailheads.

Local Transportation:

Biking: Grand Junction has an extensive biking trail system, including the Colorado Riverfront Trail. If you want to get around the city or to nearby parks, biking is a great alternative to driving.

Public Transit: The Grand Valley Transit system operates buses that run routes throughout the city, including to the Colorado National Monument and some trailheads. However, if you plan to visit more remote trails, renting a car is recommended.

Rideshare: Services like Uber and Lyft are available in Grand Junction, providing convenient access to trailheads, hotels, and nearby attractions.

Where to Stay: Hiker-Friendly Hotels, Campgrounds & RV Parks

When it comes to accommodations in Grand Junction, you'll find a variety of options that cater to hikers and outdoor enthusiasts. Whether you prefer to camp under the stars, park your RV near your favorite trail, or relax at a comfortable hotel after a day of hiking, there's something for every type of traveler.

Hotels & Lodging:

The Courtyard by Marriott Grand Junction: A modern hotel with great amenities, including an outdoor pool, a fitness center, and free parking. It's perfect for those who want to stay in a comfortable setting close to restaurants and shops, but still within driving distance of the **trails.**

Quality Inn Grand Junction: A budget-friendly hotel with a convenient location. This option is perfect for hikers looking for an affordable, clean, and comfortable place to rest after a long day of hiking.

Hotel Maverick: Located on the campus of Colorado Mesa University, this upscale hotel is known for its unique design and modern amenities. With a full-service restaurant and close access to the downtown area, it's a great option for travelers who want a more luxurious experience while still being near the outdoors.

Campgrounds:

Colorado National Monument Campground: This first-come, first-served campground offers amazing views of the surrounding canyons and is conveniently located near many of the monument's trails. It's a popular spot, so arrive early to secure a spot.

Highline Lake State Park: For a more remote camping experience, Highline Lake offers great camping spots for those looking to enjoy water activities as well as hiking. It's a great location for hiking around the lake or exploring the nearby Book Cliffs.

RV Parks:

Grand Junction KOA: This well-maintained RV park offers full hookups, a swimming pool, and is just a short drive away from some of Grand Junction's best hiking trails. It's perfect for those looking for an RV-friendly accommodation while still having access to the outdoors.

Fruitvale RV Park: A more tranquil option located near the Colorado River. It's a quieter spot, ideal for those looking to rest in between hikes while still having easy access to the town and trails.

Whether you're looking for a cozy hotel, a rustic camping experience, or an RV park with all the amenities, Grand Junction offers a range of options to suit every hiker's needs. No matter where you stay, you'll be close to the beautiful trails that make this region so special.

Packing Smart: Essential Gear, Clothing & Safety Items

When preparing for a hiking adventure in Grand Junction, packing the right gear is crucial for your safety and comfort. The unique desert and mountainous terrain means that a well-thought-out pack can make the difference between an enjoyable hike and a challenging, uncomfortable one. Here's a detailed list of the essential gear, clothing, and safety items you'll need for your journey.

Essential Gear

Backpack: A daypack or a hydration pack is ideal for most hikes around Grand Junction. Look for one that fits comfortably, has adjustable straps, and provides good airflow to avoid sweaty backs. A capacity of 15 to 30 liters should be enough for a day hike.

Navigation Tools: Always carry a topographic map or a GPS device. Cell phone reception can be spotty in some of the more remote areas, so it's important to have offline navigation tools. A compass is also a good backup.

Water Bottles & Hydration System: Staying hydrated is key when hiking in Grand Junction's dry climate. Carry enough water for your entire hike, especially if you're heading into more remote areas. A hydration reservoir (**like a Camelbak**) or multiple water bottles are essential. In summer, aim for 2 to 3 liters per person.

First Aid Kit: A compact first aid kit should include bandages, antiseptic wipes, blister treatment, pain relievers, and any personal medications. You may also want to pack tweezers for removing ticks, sunscreen, and lip balm with SPF.

Multi-tool: A multi-tool (with a knife, scissors, and pliers) can come in handy for a variety of situations, whether you need to fix your gear or handle an unexpected emergency.

Clothing

Breathable Layers: The key to staying comfortable on a hike in Grand Junction is dressing in layers. During the day, temperatures can soar, but early mornings and evenings can be quite chilly. A breathable, moisture-wicking base layer is important, followed by an insulating layer (like a fleece or light jacket), and a windbreaker or rain jacket for unpredictable weather.

Hiking Pants/Shorts: Quick-drying pants or convertible shorts are ideal, as they provide flexibility for varying temperatures. Consider UV-protective clothing if you're hiking in exposed areas during midday heat.

Hiking Boots: Invest in sturdy, comfortable hiking boots with good ankle support. If you're tackling rocky or uneven terrain, choose boots with a rubber sole and good tread for traction. Don't forget wool or moisture-wicking socks to prevent blisters.

Hat & Sunglasses: The Colorado sun can be intense, so wear a wide-brimmed hat for sun protection and polarized sunglasses to reduce glare and protect your eyes.

Gaiters: If you plan to hike during the wetter months or on trails with a lot of loose debris, gaiters can protect your boots and legs from dirt, mud, or even snakes.

Safety Items

Headlamp/Flashlight: Even if you don't plan to hike in the dark, it's important to carry a headlamp or flashlight. Always bring extra batteries, as you never know when you might need extra light.

Whistle: A whistle is a simple but effective signaling device in case of emergency. It's lightweight and easy to carry on a pack strap.

Trekking Poles: If you're tackling steep or uneven terrain, trekking poles can help reduce strain on your knees and provide extra stability.

By packing these essentials, you'll be well-prepared to take on the rugged trails of Grand Junction, whether you're heading into the Colorado National Monument or the more remote Book Cliffs.

Weather & Trail Conditions: What You Need to Know Before Heading Out

Grand Junction's diverse terrain and climate require hikers to stay informed about weather patterns and trail conditions before setting out. The region can experience rapid shifts in temperature, unexpected storms, and diverse weather conditions depending on elevation and season. Here's what you need to know:

Weather Considerations

Desert Heat: The high desert around Grand Junction can be incredibly hot in summer.

Temperatures in the desert often exceed 90°F (32°C), especially from June through August. It's vital to start your hike early in the morning or later in the evening to avoid the worst of the heat.

Mountain Temperatures: While the desert can be sweltering, the nearby Grand Mesa offers a cooler escape. In the mountains, temperatures can be 20-30°F cooler than in the desert, even during summer. Prepare for cooler temperatures at higher elevations, especially in the spring and fall.

Thunderstorms: In the summer months, thunderstorms are common in the afternoons, particularly in the mountains. These storms can develop quickly, bringing lightning, rain, and strong winds. Always check the weather forecast before heading out and be prepared to turn back if the skies start to darken.

Winter Conditions: While winter temperatures in the lowlands can be mild, higher altitudes on the Grand Mesa and Book Cliffs may have snow and ice. Conditions can be slippery, so traction devices or microspikes are a good idea in winter months.

Trail Conditions

Before setting out on any trail, be sure to check current trail conditions. Some of the popular trails, especially in the Colorado National Monument, can be affected by weather or maintenance. Trail closures and detours may happen due to flooding, erosion, or wildfires, so it's important to stay informed.

Colorado National Monument Trails: The trails in the Monument Canyon area can be impacted by rain, which makes the rocks slippery. During the spring months, trail erosion may occur after heavy storms.

Grand Mesa Trails: In winter, snow can make the trails more difficult, but they are usually open for hiking. The Grand Mesa Trail and Mesa Creek Trail are both popular year-round trails but may require snow gear in colder months.

Book Cliffs Trails: This area has rougher terrain, and trail conditions can be affected by loose rock and steep climbs. It's important to wear proper hiking boots for good traction, especially after rain when trails may be muddy.

Before heading out, consult trail resources, such as the Colorado Plateau website, **AllTrails**, or local ranger stations, for the most up-to-date trail conditions. It's always safer to check ahead to avoid disruptions and ensure a safe, enjoyable hike.

Local Rules & Permits: Avoiding Fines & Trail Closures

When hiking in Grand Junction, it's crucial to follow local rules and regulations to preserve the beauty of the area and ensure the safety of all hikers. Failure to follow these rules can result in fines, trail closures, or even accidents. Here's what you need to know:

Permits

Colorado National Monument: While most of the trails here are open to the public, you may need a $25 vehicle entry fee to access the park. Some special activities, like backcountry camping or group hikes, may require a permit. Be sure to check with the park service for specific requirements.

State Parks: Some state parks, such as Highline Lake State Park, charge a small entrance fee, generally around $7 per vehicle. If you plan to camp or boat, additional fees may apply, and a camping reservation may be required during peak seasons.

Camping Permits: While most campgrounds in Grand Junction are on a first-come, first-served basis, some areas may require a backcountry camping permit. Always check with the Bureau of Land Management (BLM) or Colorado Parks and Wildlife for specific rules on camping, especially in more remote regions.

Trail Rules & Etiquette

Stay on Marked Trails: One of thec most important rules in Grand Junction's wilderness areas is to stay on marked trails. This protects the fragile desert ecosystem and minimizes erosion.

Leave No Trace: Follow the Leave No Trace principles: pack out all trash, avoid disturbing wildlife, and leave the environment as you found it. This includes picking up pet waste and staying on established trails to reduce the impact on natural habitats.

Respect Other Hikers: Always yield to others on the trail, particularly uphill hikers, and be courteous when passing. If you're hiking with dogs, make sure they are on a leash to keep them under control and prevent them from disturbing wildlife.

Fire Regulations: Open fires are typically prohibited in many wilderness areas, including Colorado National Monument and Highline Lake State Park. If campfires are allowed, ensure you use designated fire rings and always extinguish your fire completely before leaving.

By adhering to these guidelines, you not only ensure a safer and more enjoyable hiking experience for yourself but also help protect the pristine landscapes of Grand Junction for future generations.

Chapter

3

Finding The Perfect Trail: What You Need To Know

Grand Junction offers a diverse range of hiking trails, each with its own unique appeal, but with so many options, how do you choose the perfect one for your skill level, interests, and goals? Whether you're seeking panoramic views, challenging climbs, or a peaceful walk through nature, understanding what each trail offers is essential. Here's what you need to know when searching for the perfect hiking trail.

Types of Trails in Grand Junction

Desert Trails: The high desert surrounding Grand Junction offers a variety of trails, from the iconic Colorado National Monument with its canyon views to the expansive Book Cliffs. These trails often feature rocky terrain, dry conditions, and sweeping vistas. Some are short and accessible, while others require more endurance and technical skills.

Mountain Trails: If you're looking for cooler temperatures or higher altitudes, the Grand Mesa offers a stunning change of scenery with alpine forests, lakes, and meadows. Here you'll find trails that lead through higher elevations and offer unique wildlife viewing and wildflower blooms during summer.

River Trails: The Colorado River winds through the area, offering riverside trails perfect for a peaceful hike. The Riverfront Trail is an easy, family-friendly trail that follows the river through the heart of Grand Junction, offering scenic views, wildlife sightings, and easy access for all levels of hikers.

Backcountry Trails: For the more adventurous hiker, Grand Junction has a number of backcountry trails in more remote areas, such as the Tabeguache Trail.

These trails often require a combination of navigational skills and physical endurance, but reward hikers with solitude and pristine landscapes.

Trail Length & Time Considerations

When selecting a trail, consider both its length and the time required to complete it. A short, moderate trail might take anywhere from 2 to 3 hours, while a longer and more challenging trail could take upwards of 6 to 8 hours or even an entire day. Make sure to check trail maps and estimated times for each trail to gauge how much time you'll need to allocate for the hike.

Consider Your Skill Level and Fitness

Everyone has different expectations and abilities when it comes to hiking, so it's essential to pick trails that match your physical fitness and hiking experience. Some of the more technical trails in Grand Junction require previous hiking experience and a higher level of endurance, while others are more accessible for beginners or families.

How Trails Are Rated: Understanding Easy, Moderate & Difficult Ratings

Trails in Grand Junction, like those throughout the hiking world, are rated by their difficulty to help hikers choose the right trail for their abilities. These ratings give an indication of the terrain, elevation gain, distance, and overall physical demands of the hike. Here's a breakdown of what you can expect from each difficulty level:

Easy Trails

Distance: Typically 1 to 3 miles (1.6 to 4.8 km).

Elevation Gain: Minimal to no elevation gain (less than 500 feet/150 meters).

Terrain: Mostly flat or gently rolling terrain, well-maintained paths with little to no obstacles.

Time: Generally 1 to 2 hours.

Who It's For: These trails are perfect for beginners, families, or anyone seeking a relaxing walk in nature without much physical challenge. Easy trails are usually well-marked and accessible.

For example, the Riverfront Trail in Grand Junction is an easy, family-friendly trail that runs along the Colorado River, offering picturesque views with minimal elevation.

Moderate Trails

Distance: 3 to 6 miles (4.8 to 9.6 km).

Elevation Gain: Moderate elevation gain (500 to 1,500 feet/150 to 450 meters).

Terrain: These trails may include rocky terrain, some steep sections, and uneven footing. Expect a mix of uphill and downhill sections, sometimes requiring scrambling or careful footing.

Time: Typically 2 to 5 hours.

Who It's For: Moderate trails are ideal for those with a basic fitness level or who have some hiking experience. They provide a more challenging experience without being overly strenuous.

A moderate trail example in Grand Junction is **Kokopelli Trail**, which offers beautiful views of canyons and cliffs with a moderate ascent and technical sections.

Difficult Trails

Distance: 6+ miles (9.6 km and beyond).

Elevation Gain: Steep ascents (1,500 feet/450 meters and above) and sometimes uneven, rugged terrain.

Terrain: Expect rough terrain, boulders, loose rocks, and challenging uphill or downhill sections. These trails often have technical parts, requiring a good level of fitness, stamina, and experience.

Time: Often 4 hours or more.

Who It's For: Difficult trails are best suited for experienced hikers in good physical condition. They require mental toughness, a high level of endurance, and the ability to navigate difficult terrain.

The **Tabeguache Trail** offers a challenging, remote backcountry experience that demands not only physical strength but also good navigational skills.

Altitude & Acclimatization: How to Avoid Altitude Sickness

Grand Junction sits at an elevation of approximately 4,500 feet (1,372 meters), but many of the area's trails climb higher, especially those on the Grand Mesa or the Book Cliffs. Hikers may encounter higher altitudes, and altitude sickness can become a concern for those not accustomed to it. Here's how to prepare and minimize the risk of altitude sickness:

What Is Altitude Sickness?

Altitude sickness (or acute mountain sickness, AMS) occurs when you ascend too quickly to higher altitudes, and your body doesn't have enough time to adjust to the reduced oxygen levels. Symptoms include dizziness, nausea, headaches, and shortness of breath. More severe side effects, such as high-altitude cerebral edema (HACE) or high-altitude pulmonary edema (HAPE), may result in extreme circumstances.

Preventing Altitude Sickness

Ascend Gradually: If you plan on hiking to higher altitudes, give yourself time to acclimatize. Avoid rapid elevation gain, and take it slow when you start your hike. Spend a day or two at lower elevations before tackling high-altitude hikes if possible.

Hydrate: Dehydration can exacerbate the symptoms of altitude sickness, so it's crucial to drink plenty of water before, during, and after your hike. In higher altitudes, you'll likely need more water than usual.

Take Breaks: Stop frequently to catch your breath and rest. Don't push yourself too hard during the first few hours, especially when hiking above 6,000 feet (1,800 meters).

Know the Symptoms: Be aware of the signs of altitude sickness, such as headaches, dizziness, nausea, or fatigue. If you begin experiencing symptoms, descend to a lower altitude immediately. Don't attempt to push through.

Avoid Alcohol and Smoking: Both can aggravate the effects of altitude sickness by impairing oxygen absorption and decreasing circulation.

By taking it slow, staying hydrated, and allowing your body time to adjust to higher elevations, you can minimize the risk of altitude sickness and enjoy Grand Junction's incredible hiking experiences safely. If in doubt, always opt for a moderate trail at a lower elevation before tackling those higher climbs.

Best Trails by Type:

Grand Junction is a hiker's paradise, offering a variety of trails that cater to all levels of experience and physical fitness. Whether you're looking for a short family outing, a moderate half-day adventure, or a challenging multi-day trek, Grand Junction has something for everyone. Below, we break down the best trails by type to help you choose the right one for your adventure.

Short & Scenic Hikes (Under 3 Miles, Family-Friendly)

For those who want to enjoy the beauty of the area without committing to a long trek, short and scenic hikes are the perfect choice. These hikes are usually family-friendly, offering relatively easy terrain, manageable distances, and stunning views.

Top Short Trails:

Riverfront Trail: A 2.5-mile (4 km) paved path, this trail is perfect for beginners or families with children. It winds along the Colorado River, offering scenic views of the riverbanks, nearby parks, and the surrounding landscape. The flat terrain makes it accessible to walkers, joggers, and cyclists.

McInnis Canyons Conservation Area: One of the best spots for short hikes near Grand Junction, the Turtle Rock Trail is a 2.2-mile (3.5 km) easy loop with impressive views of the Colorado River and the surrounding desert cliffs. It's a great way to explore the canyons without exerting too much effort.

Colorado National Monument – Window Rock Trail: This 1.5-mile (2.4 km) trail leads to a stunning natural rock formation that frames the distant valley below. It's a relatively easy hike with little elevation gain, making it a great choice for families or beginner hikers.

These trails provide a quick and rewarding experience, offering scenic beauty without the physical strain of longer hikes.

Half-Day Adventures (3–6 Miles, Moderate Effort)

For those looking for a bit more of a challenge but still manageable in a few hours, half-day hikes are perfect. These hikes range from 3 to 6 miles in length and offer moderate elevation gain. While still family-friendly, they will require a bit more stamina and effort.

Top Half-Day Trails:

Kokopelli Trail: This trail, which runs for over 140 miles, offers a number of smaller, accessible sections, but the 3.5-mile (5.6 km) stretch through the desert is an excellent moderate hike. It gives hikers a taste of the rugged terrain and sweeping views that Grand Junction is famous for. Be prepared for rocky paths and a bit of elevation gain.

Monument Canyon Trail: A 3.6-mile (5.8 km) moderate trail that takes you through the dramatic landscape of Colorado National Monument. You'll traverse canyons and enjoy fantastic views of the surrounding mesas. The trail features some rocky areas and a gradual incline but is well-marked and accessible to most hikers.

Tabeguache Trail (Lower Section): A 4.5-mile (7.2 km) section of the longer Tabeguache Trail, this hike provides sweeping views and a little more elevation change. As a moderate trail, it offers a nice mix of rugged terrain and enjoyable scenery, making it an ideal half-day outing.

These trails are great for hikers who are looking to stretch their legs and experience a deeper sense of adventure but don't have the time for a full-day excursion.

Full-Day Challenges (6+ Miles, Strenuous but Rewarding)

For the seasoned hiker who wants to push their limits, full-day hikes are a fantastic choice. These trails typically exceed 6 miles and involve significant elevation gain, rougher terrain, and more technical challenges. However, the rewards are well worth the effort, with breathtaking views, solitude, and a deep sense of accomplishment.

Top Full-Day Trails:

Grand Mesa – Crag Crest Trail: This 9-mile (14.5 km) trail on Grand Mesa offers hikers an exceptional backcountry experience with high-altitude views of the Western Slope and Colorado Plateau. You'll hike through alpine forests, meadows, and rocky ridgelines, with a moderate to steep incline along the way. It's a strenuous hike, but the panoramic views and unique terrain make it worth the challenge.

Colorado National Monument – Liberty Cap Trail: The 6.5-mile (10.4 km) Liberty Cap Trail takes you up to one of the park's most iconic features, Liberty Cap, offering sweeping views of the entire national monument. The trail features a steady ascent and a rocky, uneven surface. Expect a rigorous challenge, especially as you approach the summit.

Tabeguache Trail (Upper Section): The Tabeguache Trail reaches 20 miles (32 km) in total, with the upper section offering a challenging, full-day trek. This trail is perfect for seasoned hikers looking for rugged terrain, technical elements, and remote solitude. You'll encounter high desert landscapes, rocky ascents, and sweeping vistas.

These trails require proper preparation, a high level of fitness, and the ability to tackle steep ascents and variable terrain. They are for those seeking a challenging, rewarding day in the wilderness.

Multi-Day Treks & Backpacking Routes (For Serious Hikers Only)

For the true adventurer who wants to fully immerse themselves in Grand Junction's wilderness, multi-day treks are the ultimate challenge. These routes go beyond a single day's hike, requiring careful planning, backcountry navigation, and overnight camping. These trails are for experienced hikers who are comfortable carrying a heavy pack and navigating remote areas.

Top Multi-Day Trails:

Tabeguache Trail: The Tabeguache Trail is an incredible multi-day backpacking route for serious hikers. Stretching over 140 miles, this trail takes you through the heart of the rugged Colorado Plateau, with stunning vistas, remote canyons, and diverse ecosystems. Hikers can break the trail into multiple sections, each offering a different experience, from rocky desert terrain to lush meadows.

Grand Mesa Loop: The Grand Mesa Loop offers a challenging multi-day adventure for experienced hikers. This loop covers about 50 miles, winding through alpine meadows, lakes, and dense forests. With over 10,000 feet of elevation change, it offers a full backpacking experience, including the chance to camp in the pristine wilderness of the Grand Mesa.

Rimrock Trail: The Rimrock Trail provides a more rugged, backcountry hiking experience. Stretching over 50 miles, this trail offers secluded campsites, incredible mountain views, and a sense of true wilderness. As a multi-day hike, it's a challenging trek that takes hikers through deep canyons and up to towering ridgelines.

Multi-day hikes require advanced planning, including obtaining the necessary permits, carrying sufficient supplies, and making sure you're prepared for a more isolated, physically demanding experience. These treks offer the ultimate sense of adventure and a chance to explore the wild, untouched beauty of Grand Junction at a deeper level.

Choosing the Right Trail for You

Ultimately, choosing the right trail comes down to your experience level, time constraints, and the type of adventure you seek.

Grand Junction offers a diverse range of trails, so you can always find one that matches your goals. Whether you're out for a short scenic jaunt or tackling a multi-day backcountry adventure, there's no wrong choice—only the perfect one for you. Always consider your fitness level, prepare properly, and be ready to enjoy everything that this stunning destination has to offer.

Wildlife & Plants: What You Might Encounter on the Trails

One of the highlights of hiking in Grand Junction is the rich biodiversity that you'll encounter on the trails. The region's varied terrain—ranging from high desert to alpine forests—hosts an impressive array of wildlife and plant life. Whether you're an avid nature lover or a casual hiker, keep your eyes peeled for the incredible creatures and flora that call this area home.

Wildlife to Watch for:

Mammals: The area is home to a diverse collection of mammals, including mule deer, rocky mountain elk, and black bears. While bear sightings are relatively rare, it's important to take precautions by storing food properly and making noise while hiking to avoid surprising these creatures. Coyotes and foxes are also commonly seen in the early morning or late evening, while smaller mammals like chipmunks, squirrels, and rabbits scurry across the trails.

Birds: Grand Junction offers great birdwatching opportunities. You might encounter red-tailed hawks, golden eagles, and American kestrels soaring above the cliffs. The area is also home to a wide variety of songbirds such as mountain bluebirds and western meadowlarks.

Bird lovers will appreciate the range of species, especially in the spring and summer months when migration brings new arrivals.

Reptiles & Amphibians: Be prepared for sightings of desert reptiles such as Western fence lizards, Gila monsters, and rattlesnakes. While rattlesnakes are venomous, they typically give a warning rattle before striking and will avoid human interaction if given the chance. You may also encounter toads, frogs, and salamanders in the cooler, wet areas of the trails.

Insects: From grasshoppers to butterflies, the insect life in Grand Junction can be fascinating to observe. You'll also find beetles, dragonflies, and moths throughout the summer months, with some species playing vital roles in pollination.

Plants to Observe:

The trails in Grand Junction are adorned with a variety of native plants, ranging from hardy desert cacti to lush alpine meadows. Some key plant species to look out for include:

Cacti & Succulents: Prickly pear cactus, cholla, and barrel cactus are common in the desert landscapes. These hardy plants thrive in the arid conditions and provide stunning flowers in the spring.

Wildflowers: Depending on the season, you may see Indian paintbrush, lupines, and bluebells dotting the landscape with color. Bitterbrush and sagebrush dominate the semi-desert zones, while wild roses and columbine add to the beauty in higher elevations.

Trees & Shrubs: The higher elevations are home to ponderosa pines, Aspen trees, and oakbrush. Near water sources, you'll encounter willows, cottonwoods, and junipers, all of which provide shade and habitat for wildlife.

While hiking, be mindful of your surroundings and respect the plants and animals. Avoid disturbing the wildlife, and don't pick or trample the plants, as they play a vital role in maintaining the ecosystem.

Hiking with Kids & Dogs: Trails That Are Safe & Fun for Everyone

Grand Junction's hiking trails are not only perfect for experienced adventurers but also for families and pet owners looking to share the joy of the outdoors. Whether you're bringing your kids or your four-legged friend along, there are plenty of trails designed to be fun, safe, and easy for all members of the family.

Hiking with Kids:

When hiking with children, it's important to select trails that are manageable in length and offer a variety of interesting features to keep them engaged. Fortunately, Grand Junction has a number of family-friendly hikes that feature gentle terrain, scenic views, and exciting natural elements.

Botanical Gardens Trail: This easy 1.5-mile (2.4 km) loop in the Grand Junction Botanic Gardens offers families a leisurely walk through lush gardens and vibrant plant life. With plenty of benches to take breaks and a beautiful setting, it's a great trail for young children to enjoy.

James M. Robb – Colorado River State Park: With several short, well-maintained trails, this park is ideal for families with kids. The trails range from easy 1–2 mile walks to longer hikes, all featuring scenic views of the river, wildlife, and open meadows.

The flat terrain makes it an excellent choice for strollers and young hikers.

Rabbit Valley Trail: This 3-mile (4.8 km) trail offers gentle ascents and panoramic views of the desert landscape, making it a great choice for kids to explore the wonders of the high desert without feeling overwhelmed by the terrain.

Hiking with Dogs:

Grand Junction is incredibly dog-friendly, with many trails that welcome pets on a leash. However, it's essential to keep your dog on the trail and be mindful of wildlife and plant life, which can sometimes be harmful to animals.

Rim Rock Drive: This popular trail offers several scenic, dog-friendly options where you and your dog can enjoy beautiful views of the Colorado National Monument. Just remember to carry extra water for your dog and keep them on a leash, as the area can get hot during summer months.

North Fruita Desert: Known for its expansive trails, the North Fruita Desert offers several dog-friendly options, including flat, easy-to-navigate paths that allow your dog to explore the open space. These trails are perfect for a longer, more relaxed hike.

Colorado Riverfront Trail: If you're looking for a scenic stroll by the water, the Colorado Riverfront Trail is a great spot for dogs. The flat terrain is perfect for pets, and the lush riverside environment provides plenty of opportunities for exploration.

Before heading out, make sure to check trail regulations, and always bring enough water, dog waste bags, and sunscreen for both you and your pup.

How to Avoid Disappointment: What Photos Don't Tell You About Grand Junction's Trails (Prevents Unrealistic Expectations from Instagram-Perfect Images)

With the rise of social media and Instagram, it's easy to develop unrealistic expectations when it comes to outdoor adventures. The photos you see online are often edited, cropped, and staged to look perfect, which can lead to disappointment when your experience doesn't match what you saw on your feed.

The Realities of Grand Junction's Trails:

The Terrain Can Be Rugged: While many Instagram images show stunning panoramic views, it's important to remember that the trails in Grand Junction can be rugged and challenging. You may encounter steep ascents, loose rocks, and uneven footing that are not always visible in photos. Make sure to check trail difficulty and prepare for the actual terrain you'll face.

Weather Conditions Can Be Unpredictable: Photos of perfectly clear skies and sunshine may give the impression that the weather is always perfect, but Grand Junction's weather can change quickly, especially in higher elevations. Always check the forecast before heading out, and be prepared for sudden weather shifts, including rain, strong winds, or temperature drops.

Distance and Scale Are Often Misleading: Photos can make trails appear much shorter or easier than they actually are. An image of a beautiful rock formation might be taken from a vantage point that makes it seem closer than it really is.

Ensure you're aware of the trail's length and elevation gain before embarking on your hike.

Expect Some Crowds: The popular trails near Grand Junction, especially those with stunning views, can get crowded, particularly during peak seasons. If you're looking for solitude or a more serene experience, consider exploring lesser-known trails or heading out early in the morning.

By managing your expectations and preparing for the realities of hiking in Grand Junction, you'll have a more enjoyable experience and avoid the frustration that can come with unrealistic expectations from those "Instagram-perfect" images.

Chapter

4

Best Hikes In Grand Junction

Grand Junction is home to a diverse range of hiking trails that offer something for everyone. From easy, family-friendly walks to challenging hikes that reward you with breathtaking views, the area caters to all skill levels. Whether you're looking for a peaceful stroll along the Colorado River or an adventurous climb up the rocky ridges, Grand Junction's trails will not disappoint. Below are some of the best hikes that showcase the region's natural beauty.

EASY & FAMILY-FRIENDLY TRAILS

For those who want to take in the stunning scenery without committing to a strenuous trek, Grand Junction has several easy and family-friendly trails that offer incredible views, interesting geology, and the chance to encounter local wildlife. These trails are ideal for those with young children or those just looking for a relaxing day outdoors.

Devils Kitchen Trail – Amazing Rock Formations in a Short Hike

The Devils Kitchen Trail is an absolute gem for those wanting to experience the grandeur of Grand Junction's natural rock formations without exerting too much energy. This 1.5-mile loop offers a quick but rewarding hike that showcases the area's unique geology.

As you wander along this well-maintained trail, you'll encounter dramatic red rock formations and towering sandstone spires, creating a surreal, otherworldly landscape. The highlight of the hike is the Devil's Kitchen, a fascinating rock alcove surrounded by towering cliffs, which is a perfect spot to stop and marvel at the rugged beauty of the region.

This trail is family-friendly, making it perfect for children or anyone looking for a scenic, short hike that doesn't require a full day of effort. The trail is easy to follow with moderate elevation gain, making it an accessible option for beginners or those who want to enjoy a relaxed walk while exploring one of Grand Junction's most unique landscapes.

Pro Tip: Bring along a camera to capture the incredible rock formations and panoramic views of the surrounding desert landscape. It's a great spot for photos and a peaceful place to stop for a break.

Dinosaur Hill Trail – A Walk Through Prehistoric History

If you have young dinosaur enthusiasts in your family, the Dinosaur Hill Trail is an unmissable experience. This 1.5-mile trail offers a fantastic introduction to Grand Junction's prehistoric past, and it's one of the most exciting family-friendly hikes in the area.

The trail itself is short and easy, with minimal elevation gain, making it perfect for young children or first-time hikers. As you hike along the dirt path, you'll pass signs and exhibits that explain the area's rich dinosaur history, providing educational content for all ages. The trail takes you to the top of Dinosaur Hill, where you'll find fantastic views of the Colorado River, the surrounding valley, and the Book Cliffs.

In addition to the fossil-related exhibits, you might even stumble across some fossilized footprints—reminders of the dinosaurs that once roamed this land millions of years ago.

Pro Tip: Visit the Dinosaur Journey Museum before or after your hike to learn even more about the fossil discoveries in the region. It's a great way to round off the experience.

Riverfront Trail – Relaxing Views Along the Colorado River

For those who prefer a peaceful riverside stroll, the Riverfront Trail is the perfect choice. This 6-mile paved path follows the winding course of the Colorado River and offers stunning views of the water, local wildlife, and surrounding landscapes. Whether you're walking, running, or biking, the Riverfront Trail is an ideal spot to enjoy the serenity of nature without venturing too far from the city.

Along the way, you'll find shaded areas, picnic spots, and benches where you can stop and rest while watching kayakers and paddleboarders navigate the river. The trail is very accessible with mostly flat terrain, making it an excellent choice for families, beginners, or anyone looking for a leisurely hike.

For nature lovers, the wildlife along the trail is abundant. You might encounter bald eagles, waterfowl, and various river otters, making it a great trail for birdwatching. The trail also winds through the Rimrock Natural Area, offering picturesque views of the Book Cliffs.

Pro Tip: The Riverfront Trail connects to other trails in the area, so it's easy to extend your hike if you wish. You can also enjoy kayaking or fishing along the river, making this a versatile outdoor adventure.

Miramonte Rim Trail – Easy Trail with Panoramic Views

For those seeking an easy hike with a touch of adventure, the Miramonte Rim Trail is a fantastic option. This 3.5-mile loop provides stunning panoramic views of Grand Junction, the Book Cliffs, and the Colorado River, all while remaining relatively easy to navigate.

The trail is a perfect introduction to the area's landscapes, offering sweeping vistas and a moderate incline that's suitable for beginners or families with older children. Along the way, you'll hike through high desert terrain and sagebrush, with a few shaded areas that provide relief during the warmer months. The vistas at the top are worth every step of the journey, making this an ideal spot for photographers or those looking to take in the breathtaking scenery.

While the hike may be short, the views from the rim are expansive, giving you a chance to truly appreciate the diverse landscapes that define Grand Junction. The trail also offers a great opportunity for wildlife watching, so keep your eyes open for deer, rabbits, and various bird species.

Pro Tip: Bring a pair of binoculars for better views of the distant cliffs and wildlife. The Miramonte Rim Trail is especially beautiful during sunrise and sunset, so consider timing your hike for one of these golden hours.

Liberty Cap Trail (Lower Section) – A Beginner-Friendly Rock Climb

For a bit more of a challenge without going overboard, the Liberty Cap Trail (**Lower Section**) offers a beginner-friendly rock climb that will test your skills without overwhelming you. The lower section of this trail is perfect for those looking to try out a simple rock scramble, as it introduces hikers to a bit of technical climbing without requiring advanced skills or gear.

The 2-**mile** trail takes you through open desert landscapes before reaching the base of Liberty Cap, a distinctive rock formation that stands out among the surrounding cliffs. The lower section offers a gentle ascent with some minor scrambling required, allowing hikers to test their rock-climbing abilities in a safe, controlled environment.

The views from the top of Liberty Cap are truly stunning, with panoramic vistas of the Colorado River, **Redlands**, and the Book **Cliffs**. The upper section of the trail is more challenging, but even if you choose to stop halfway, you'll still experience plenty of beautiful scenery.

Pro Tip: Wear sturdy footwear with good grip, as the rock can be slippery in places. This trail is ideal for those looking to try rock climbing for the first time or those seeking an adventure that's just a little more demanding than a typical hike.

Grand Junction offers a wonderful mix of easy and family-friendly trails, with something to suit every hiker.

Whether you're in search of prehistoric history, scenic views along the river, or a short adventure with panoramic vistas, these trails provide great opportunities to explore and enjoy the natural beauty of the area. Each one is accessible, rewarding, and designed to give you a memorable experience.

Chapter

5

MODERATE TRAILS (For Adventurous Hikers)

For hikers who are ready to take on a bit more of a challenge, moderate trails offer the perfect balance of adventure and stunning landscapes. These trails are ideal for those who have hiked a bit before and are looking to step up their experience without committing to a strenuous, all-day trek. Grand Junction's moderate trails provide diverse terrain, beautiful vistas, and a great opportunity to test your skills while enjoying the region's natural beauty.

Serpents Trail – The "Crookedest Road" Now a Stunning Hike

One of the most iconic and serpentine hikes in Grand Junction, the Serpents Trail offers a unique and thrilling experience for moderate hikers. Once a historic road with the title of the **"crookedest road,"** this trail has been transformed into a hiking route that winds its way up through the hills, providing jaw-dropping views of the surrounding desert landscape.

The 2.5-mile trail features a series of switchbacks that make the climb feel like a constant zig-zagging motion, which is not only physically engaging but also visually stimulating as the views change with each curve. As you ascend, you'll be treated to expansive vistas of the Colorado River and the Book Cliffs—making every step feel worthwhile.

The terrain ranges from rocky sections to more sandy stretches, and the elevation gain is moderate, offering a good workout without being too overwhelming.

The real magic of Serpents Trail lies in the panoramic views you'll encounter as you approach the summit.

At the top, you're rewarded with a breathtaking perspective of Grand Junction and the surrounding areas, including a view of Monument Canyon and the Grand Mesa. The trail offers the perfect balance of exercise and scenic beauty, and it's a great option for those who want to take in both the views and the history of the land.

Pro Tip: Since this trail is moderately steep in some sections, be sure to wear sturdy shoes with good traction. Make sure to carry plenty of water, especially during the warmer months, and take your time during the climb to enjoy the changing scenery. Sunrise or sunset hikes are especially stunning on this trail, as the light transforms the landscape.

No Thoroughfare Canyon – Hidden Waterfalls & Stunning Rock Walls

For those seeking a bit more seclusion and a peaceful adventure, the No Thoroughfare Canyon trail is an absolute must. This 5-mile hike takes you deep into one of the more hidden gems of the Grand Junction area, showcasing an amazing diversity of waterfalls, rock walls, and lush greenery that contrasts with the surrounding desert environment. The hike is moderate in difficulty, with a well-marked path and some uneven terrain that makes it a bit more adventurous without being overwhelming.

The beauty of No Thoroughfare Canyon lies in its mysterious and almost magical atmosphere. As you follow the trail along the canyon floor, you'll pass tall rock walls and massive sandstone cliffs, which tower above you on either side.

The trail weaves its way through the canyon, sometimes skirting along the edge of the creek that runs through the canyon floor, and providing natural shade from the cliffs overhead.

One of the highlights of the trail is the opportunity to witness waterfalls hidden deep within the canyon. Depending on the season, these cascading falls can range from a gentle trickle to a more dramatic water flow. In the spring, when the snowmelt swells the creek, these waterfalls are particularly spectacular.

The hike also offers opportunities for wildlife viewing, as deer, wild turkeys, and bighorn sheep are often spotted in the area. Birdwatchers will also appreciate the variety of species that make their home in the canyon, making it an excellent spot for birding.

The path is mostly shaded, making it a great option for hot summer hikes, though some sections can get tricky with loose rocks and uneven footing. The difficulty lies in maintaining a steady pace and dealing with occasional rocky sections. But for those who love to explore nature off the beaten path, No Thoroughfare Canyon is a hike you won't soon forget.

Pro Tip: Wear sturdy hiking boots to help with footing in the canyon's more rocky sections. Depending on the time of year, a good hat and sunscreen are essential as some parts of the trail lack cover, while others are shaded. The waterfall sections are best visited in the spring when the runoff is strongest. Always bring enough water to stay hydrated, as the heat can be intense during summer months.

Why These Trails Stand Out

Both the Serpents Trail and No Thoroughfare Canyon represent the unique appeal of Grand Junction's moderate hiking options.

While the Serpents Trail offers a more open, panoramic view with some moderate challenges in the form of switchbacks and elevation gain, No Thoroughfare Canyon presents a quieter, more serene experience with hidden waterfalls and impressive geological features. These trails are perfect for hikers who are looking to push themselves a bit further without overexerting.

Whether you're seeking the winding, serpentine road-like climb of the Serpents Trail, or the cool, shaded canyon with waterfalls and wildlife of No Thoroughfare Canyon, Grand Junction's moderate trails are full of opportunities to enjoy both the challenge and the rewards of hiking.

Mica Mine Trail – A Trail with Glittering Rocks & Mining History

For those intrigued by both natural beauty and historical intrigue, the Mica Mine Trail is a fantastic moderate hike that offers a unique combination of scenic views and a peek into Grand Junction's mining past. This 3.5-mile trail winds its way through a mix of desert landscapes, rugged terrain, and remnants of old mining operations, making it an excellent choice for history buffs and nature lovers alike.

The **Mica Mine Trail** begins with a gradual ascent through the desert brush and continues through rocky paths as it nears the mine's site. What makes this trail stand out are the glittering mica rocks scattered along the path.

As the sun hits them, these mica crystals catch the light, giving the trail a shimmering effect that's truly mesmerizing.

These natural gems were historically mined for their reflective properties, and you may still spot a few remnants of the old mining equipment that once operated here.

Along the way, the trail also offers expansive views of the **Colorado National Monument**, with its towering red rock cliffs and expansive canyons. The combination of desert flora and geological wonders makes this trail not only a moderate challenge but also a journey through the region's rich history. As you continue toward the mine itself, the remnants of the old mining shaft provide a fascinating glimpse into the past.

This hike is relatively short but offers a rewarding experience for those who enjoy combining natural beauty with a sense of history. The elevation gain is moderate, and there are a few rocky areas that require careful footing, making it an excellent choice for hikers looking for a varied and interesting trail.

Pro Tip: Wear hiking boots with good traction to navigate the rocky parts of the trail safely. Also, be sure to bring plenty of water, as the sun can make this trail quite hot, especially in summer. If you're a history enthusiast, take some time to explore the mine ruins and imagine what life would have been like for those who worked there.

Liberty Cap Trail (Full Route) – A Tougher Climb with Great Rewards

If you're an experienced hiker looking to push yourself on a tougher climb with impressive rewards at the top, the Liberty Cap Trail (Full Route) is the trail for you.

Stretching across 5.6 miles, this challenging trail offers steep ascents, rocky terrain, and breathtaking views of the surrounding desert and Grand Junction area. Known for its dramatic switchbacks and steep sections, it's a trail best suited for those who have a strong hiking foundation and are looking to take their adventure to the next level.

The trail starts with a steady incline and soon escalates into a more strenuous climb, winding up the red rock cliffs toward the iconic Liberty Cap, a prominent rock formation that marks the trail's high point. This challenging route requires stamina and careful navigation through rocky sections, but the views from the summit are truly worth every step. From the top, you can gaze over the Colorado River and the surrounding canyons, with panoramic vistas stretching for miles in every direction. The combination of rocky ridges and distant views of the Book Cliffs and Grand Mesa creates a view that's unmatched and will leave you feeling like you've conquered something special.

While the Liberty Cap Trail is a physically demanding hike, it is also a highly rewarding experience for those who seek both a physical challenge and spectacular views. As you push your way to the summit, you'll feel a true sense of accomplishment as you reach the top of the rock formation, where the views are staggering.

Pro Tip: Make sure you have a solid pair of hiking boots to help you tackle the steep climbs and rocky sections of this trail. Be sure to bring enough water and snacks to fuel your journey, and if you plan to hike during the warmer months, start early to avoid the midday heat. Take plenty of breaks to soak in the view and to rest your legs.

Echo Canyon Trail – A Trail with Pools, Waterfalls & Red Rock Walls

For hikers who enjoy a mix of water features, scenic views, and lush surroundings, the Echo Canyon Trail offers one of the most rewarding moderate hikes in Grand Junction. This 5.5-mile trail takes you deep into a stunning canyon filled with pools, waterfalls, and towering red rock walls, creating a serene environment that feels almost like a hidden oasis in the desert.

The **Echo Canyon Trail** is a wonderful blend of nature—a hike that's full of surprises, with several waterfalls and natural pools scattered along the way. Depending on the time of year, the waterfalls can be more dramatic, with the sounds of the rushing water providing a peaceful soundtrack to your hike. The canyon walls, formed by ancient rock layers, rise dramatically on either side, creating a cool, shaded atmosphere that provides relief from the desert heat.

As you make your way through the canyon, you'll also notice a variety of wildlife and plants that call the canyon home. The lush, verdant environment is a stark contrast to the surrounding desert landscape, making it a truly unique hiking experience in Grand Junction.

While the hike does involve some uphill sections, it's not as strenuous as some of the other trails in the area, making it a great choice for those who want to explore the canyon's natural beauty without committing to a longer, more difficult hike.

The waterfalls and rock walls create a serene atmosphere, making it an excellent trail for those looking to connect with nature and enjoy a beautiful day outdoors.

Pro Tip: Bring water shoes if you plan on wading into the pools or standing near the waterfalls, as the rocks can be slippery. This trail is best hiked during the spring or fall, when temperatures are moderate, and the waterfalls are most likely to be flowing. Make sure to pack plenty of water and be aware of the varying trail conditions, as some areas may be rocky or slippery after rain.

Why These Trails Are Worth the Hike

Each of these moderate trails offers something unique, whether it's the historical elements of the Mica Mine Trail, the challenging ascent of Liberty Cap, or the waterfalls and serenity found in Echo Canyon. All three of these trails highlight the diverse landscape of Grand Junction, with their varied terrain, stunning views, and opportunities for wildlife watching. Whether you're looking to challenge yourself with a steep climb, explore hidden waterfalls, or learn about the area's mining history, these trails are sure to provide a memorable experience. Each one is a perfect choice for hikers seeking adventure and beauty in equal measure.

Chapter

6

CHALLENGING TRAILS
(For Experienced Hikers)

The Monument Canyon Trail is one of the most iconic and challenging hikes in Grand Junction, ideal for experienced hikers looking for a seriously rewarding adventure. This trail is not for the faint-hearted—spanning 6.8 miles with a significant elevation gain, it requires stamina, endurance, and the ability to navigate through rugged terrain, but the payoff is well worth the effort.

What makes the Monument Canyon Trail so special is the sheer immensity and beauty of the landscape it traverses. As you begin your hike, you'll quickly find yourself surrounded by towering sandstone monoliths, some reaching up to 200 feet in height. These monumental rock formations seem to come out of nowhere, with the canyon's red and orange hues contrasting brilliantly against the blue sky. The trail offers sweeping vistas of the Colorado National Monument, with dramatic cliff faces and mesas that stretch into the horizon.

The hike itself is a difficult challenge due to the steep sections and uneven footing. The trail winds its way through a series of switchbacks, rocky outcrops, and narrow canyon corridors, which make for a technical and strenuous ascent. However, the views as you climb are breathtaking, with each turn revealing even more awe-inspiring vistas. This is not a hike for those looking for a leisurely stroll—hiking boots with good ankle support are essential, and a high level of fitness is required to handle the trail's challenges.

The highlight of the trail comes when you reach the top and look out over the canyon. From here, the panoramic views are unparalleled, allowing you to take in not only the monoliths themselves but also the surrounding high desert landscape, dotted with scattered rock formations and distant mesas.

The beauty of the landscape is truly humbling, and there's a real sense of accomplishment as you stand atop this ancient geological wonder.

Pro Tip: Start early to avoid the heat, especially in summer months, as parts of this trail are exposed with little shade. Bring plenty of water, wear sturdy hiking boots, and consider carrying a trail map—the trail can be tricky in some spots, and it's always wise to plan ahead.

Ute Canyon Trail – A True Wilderness Experience

For seasoned hikers seeking a true wilderness adventure, the Ute Canyon Trail is a must-do. This challenging, 10-mile out-and-back trail is not only one of the longest in the Grand Junction area, but it also offers an experience unlike any other, immersing hikers in the heart of rugged canyons, lush forests, and remote wilderness. The Ute Canyon Trail provides a truly untamed atmosphere, perfect for those looking to escape the crowds and explore a more isolated part of the region.

This trail is demanding both in terms of distance and terrain. The path begins at the trailhead near the Ute Canyon Overlook and immediately descends into the canyon, passing through a series of rocky ravines, creek beds, and dense vegetation. As you progress deeper into the canyon, the trail crosses over small creeks and navigates through dense thickets of piñon pine and juniper trees, offering a sense of seclusion that is hard to come by in other parts of Grand Junction.

Hikers are rewarded with stunning views of the canyon's rugged walls, towering cliffs, and the meandering creek that cuts its way through the landscape. The trail provides a perfect opportunity for experienced adventurers to immerse themselves in nature and truly disconnect from the world. While the initial descent can be steep, it's the return ascent that challenges even the most seasoned hikers. The hike back involves a gruelling climb out of the canyon, requiring strength and endurance, but the feeling of triumph at the top is unmatched.

What sets the **Ute Canyon Trail** apart is its solitude—while other trails in Grand Junction may get crowded, this one feels like a hidden gem, offering you the rare opportunity to hike through untouched wilderness. As you venture further into the canyon, you may encounter wildlife, including deer, bighorn sheep, and a variety of birds, adding to the sense of adventure.

Pro Tip: Due to the challenging nature of this trail, bring adequate supplies—plenty of water, high-energy snacks, and proper footwear are a must. The terrain can be unpredictable, so be prepared for some technical scrambling and ensure you're fit enough to handle the strenuous climb back. Start early in the morning to beat the midday heat and allow yourself plenty of time to complete the hike.

Why These Challenging Trails Are Worth the Effort

Both the Monument Canyon Trail and the Ute Canyon Trail are designed for experienced hikers looking to push their limits while soaking in some of the most stunning and diverse landscapes Grand Junction has to offer.

Whether you're drawn to the massive sandstone formations of Monument Canyon or the remote wilderness of Ute Canyon, these hikes provide the ultimate challenge, but with incredible rewards at the end. The trails require serious physical effort and mental fortitude, but for those who enjoy a challenge, these routes will leave you feeling accomplished and deeply connected to the wild beauty of the region. Fitness, preparation, and the right mindset are key to tackling these trails—and the views and sense of accomplishment that await at the top make it all worthwhile.

Rattlesnake Arches Trail – Second Largest Arch Collection in the World

The Rattlesnake Arches Trail is a must-do for anyone seeking both a challenging adventure and a visual feast, especially for those drawn to natural rock formations. Located just outside of Grand Junction, this trail is home to the second-largest collection of natural stone arches in the world, boasting over 20 stunning arches scattered throughout the rugged terrain. This 5.5-mile out-and-back hike is a true gem for experienced hikers who want to explore one of the more hidden wonders of the region.

The trail starts in a high desert landscape before ascending into a series of rugged ridges and rocky outcrops, where the arches begin to reveal themselves. The arch formations themselves are nothing short of spectacular. As you make your way along the trail, you'll come across massive sandstone arches, some of which stand over 100 feet tall, forming dramatic natural windows into the vast expanse of the Colorado Plateau.

Despite its moderate length, the trail's terrain can be challenging, especially for those not accustomed to steep inclines, loose rocks, and the occasional scramble. The most demanding section of the hike occurs as you climb toward the arches themselves, where you'll need to navigate some rocky paths and sharp switchbacks. But with every turn, you are rewarded with ever-expanding views of the surrounding desert landscape and glimpses of these awe-inspiring natural arches.

What truly sets the **Rattlesnake Arches Trail** apart from others in the region is the incredible solitude it offers. While popular landmarks like the Colorado National Monument or the Grand Mesa might draw crowds, Rattlesnake Arches remains largely undiscovered by casual hikers, providing a quiet and more intimate experience with nature. As you traverse the trail, you'll find yourself in total awe of the arches, each one seemingly more impressive than the last.

Pro Tip: Wear high-ankle hiking boots with good tread to avoid slipping on the rocky terrain. Take plenty of water, as the exposed desert sections can get hot during the day, and keep your camera handy—you'll want to capture the beauty of the arches from every angle.

Palisade Plunge – One of Grand Junction's Longest & Most Epic Trails

For adrenaline junkies and avid adventurers, the Palisade Plunge is the ultimate trail, offering one of the longest and most epic downhills in the entire Grand Junction area.

Stretching over 32 miles, the Palisade Plunge is a mountain biking trail (with some sections open to hiking) that descends from the top of the Grand Mesa to the small town of Palisade, offering a thrilling mix of technical terrain, epic views, and an unparalleled descent that's sure to challenge even the most experienced riders or hikers.

The adventure begins at the summit of Grand Mesa, at an elevation of 10,000 feet, where the trailhead offers panoramic views of the Western Slope. From here, the trail snakes its way down the mountain, descending through a variety of scenic environments— from dense aspen forests to open meadows, rugged rock formations, and remote canyons. The dramatic change in scenery as you drop elevation is one of the highlights of the Palisade Plunge, with an ever-changing landscape that captivates hikers and bikers alike.

Though primarily designed as a mountain biking trail, the Palisade Plunge offers challenging terrain for hikers looking for a strenuous, all-day journey. The trail is best known for its continuous downhill sections, which make for an exciting descent, but there are also steep sections that require caution. Expect to tackle tight switchbacks, loose gravel, and plenty of rocks and roots. For bikers, it's one of the most thrilling rides in Colorado, but hikers will find it just as engaging, though it's best to come prepared for a long day on the trail.

At the end of the 32-mile journey, you'll find yourself in Palisade, a quaint town known for its fruit orchards and wine vineyards, perfect for a post-hike celebration. Many hikers or bikers choose to celebrate their achievement by exploring the town and enjoying local wine or cider.

Pro Tip: Be prepared for the elevation drop and technical sections of the trail, especially if you're hiking. Knee protection and proper footwear are important, and make sure to pack plenty of water and snacks for the long day ahead.

Fruita Paleo Area to Pollock Bench – A Rugged, Remote Trek

The Fruita Paleo Area to Pollock Bench is one of the most remote and rugged hiking routes in the Grand Junction area, making it perfect for experienced hikers looking for a challenging trek through some of the wildest and most isolated landscapes. This 13-mile, out-and-back route offers an incredible journey through ancient fossil fields, rugged canyons, and high desert terrain, providing a true wilderness experience that few other trails in the area can match.

The hike begins at the **Fruita Paleo** Area, a spot that's significant for its fossil discoveries and rich history. As you follow the trail, you'll pass through the rugged terrain, climbing steadily toward the Pollock Bench, a high plateau that offers breathtaking views of the surrounding desert and the Colorado River. Along the way, you'll encounter a series of canyon walls, rock formations, and dry creek beds, making for a truly adventurous and remote experience. The terrain is rough, with a mixture of rocky outcrops, steep ascents, and occasional scrambling, so be prepared for a physically demanding day on the trail.

One of the major highlights of the hike is the sense of isolation. This trail is far less trafficked than many others in the Grand Junction area, offering an opportunity to connect deeply with nature and experience the wilderness without the crowds. As you make your way across the landscape, you may encounter wildlife, such as desert bighorn sheep, mule deer, or even a Golden Eagle, soaring high above.

The Pollock Bench itself offers incredible views of the surrounding desert and distant mesas. While this hike is physically demanding, the stunning scenery and the quiet solitude of the trail make it well worth the effort.

Pro Tip: Given the remote nature of this trail, make sure to bring a topographical map, extra water, and a GPS device. The hike can take a full day, so be prepared with trail snacks and proper gear, including sun protection and sturdy footwear for the rugged sections.

Each of these challenging hikes—Rattlesnake Arches, the Palisade Plunge, and the Fruita Paleo Area to Pollock Bench—offers its own distinct challenges and rewards. Whether you're drawn to the unique arches, the thrill of long descents, or the remote wilderness, Grand Junction's hiking trails cater to the most adventurous and experienced hikers. But remember, these hikes require physical endurance, preparation, and proper gear to make the most of the stunning landscapes and unique environments they offer. Always come prepared and respect the wild beauty of Grand Junction, and you'll find yourself rewarded with experiences that few others will ever have the privilege of witnessing.

Chapter

7

Multi-Day Hikes & Backpacking Adventures

Grand Junction and its surrounding areas offer some of the most spectacular multi-day hiking and backpacking routes in Colorado. These hikes give you the chance to fully immerse yourself in nature, explore remote areas, and experience the rugged beauty of the region over several days. Whether you're new to backpacking or an experienced hiker, Grand Junction has routes that cater to different skill levels and offer incredible views, diverse ecosystems, and an unforgettable adventure.

Hidden Gems: Underrated Trails That Are Worth Exploring

While popular trails like Rattlesnake Arches or the Monument Canyon Trail often steal the spotlight, Grand Junction is home to several hidden gems that are less trafficked yet equally as stunning. These lesser-known hikes offer an opportunity to escape the crowds and discover parts of the region that few have explored.

One such hidden gem is the **Little Book Cliffs Trail**, which spans approximately 20 miles of rugged terrain in the Little Book Cliffs Wild Horse Area. This trail is perfect for those looking for a remote wilderness experience, as it winds through cliff-lined canyons, over rocky plateaus, and past wild horses that roam the area. With only a few scattered campsites along the trail, this hike provides a true backcountry experience, giving hikers a chance to disconnect completely from the outside world.

Another lesser-known trail that deserves attention is the **North Fruita Desert Loop**, a multi-day backpacking route that takes you through the desert and sagebrush flats, with mesmerizing views of red rock canyons and desert landscapes.

This loop is ideal for hikers who enjoy both the isolation of the wilderness and the diversity of the terrain, as it combines challenging ascents with scenic vistas and desert beauty.

Lastly, the **Fruita Paleo Area** to Pollock Bench, while not as remote as the other options, offers an incredible backpacking route that winds through rugged rock formations and desert landscapes. Hikers will camp along remote dry creek beds and explore fossil-rich areas that make this route one of the most unique experiences Grand Junction has to offer.

These hidden gems may not have the same visibility as some of the more popular trails, but they offer a deeper and more authentic hiking experience for those looking to explore untouched wilderness.

Best Routes for a Weekend Adventure (For Those Looking for Overnight Hikes)

For hikers who are looking for a more manageable multi-day adventure over a weekend, Grand Junction offers several excellent trails that allow you to fully immerse yourself in nature without needing a week's worth of vacation time. These shorter, overnight hikes give you the chance to tackle the backcountry while enjoying an easy-going pace.

One of the best options for a weekend backpacking adventure is the **McInnis Canyons National Conservation Area**, which features the Rattlesnake Arches Trail.

This trail can be easily done over the course of two days, with plenty of opportunities to camp along the way. The first day of the hike takes you through desert landscapes with views of ancient arches, while the second day leads you to the stunning Rattlesnake Arches, where you can camp nearby and enjoy an unforgettable evening under the stars. The trail is both scenic and manageable for those with moderate experience in backpacking.

Another great choice is the **Colorado National Monument**, home to the Black Ridge Canyon Wilderness. The Black Ridge Loop Trail offers a multi-day adventure that covers over 20 miles of rugged terrain. The trail takes hikers through remote canyons, past towering sandstone formations, and across high desert plateaus. It's perfect for those who are looking to explore the wilderness while soaking in the unique landscape of the Monument. The route provides a challenging yet manageable experience, and the campsites along the way offer incredible scenic views of the surrounding rock formations.

For those looking for a weekend adventure that combines both mountainous terrain and desert beauty, the **Grand Mesa Backpacking Loop** is a fantastic choice. The loop covers roughly 20 miles of the Grand Mesa, offering the chance to explore high-altitude meadows, spruce forests, and remote lakes. While the loop can be completed over a weekend, it does present a moderate challenge, as you'll encounter significant elevation changes as you hike between the mesa's peaks and valleys. The Grand Mesa offers campsites with breathtaking views of the surrounding valleys and the distant San Juan Mountains, making it an ideal spot for hikers who want to experience the full variety of Colorado's natural beauty.

Camping on the Trail: Where to Set Up Camp & What to Pack

When backpacking in Grand Junction, camping along the trail is an integral part of the experience. Knowing where to set up camp and how to properly pack for these adventures is crucial to having a safe and enjoyable trip.

Where to Set Up Camp:

For multi-day hikes, it's essential to find campsites that are both safe and scenic, while also being legal and in accordance with local regulations. Most backpacking routes have designated campsites, although there are some that require backcountry camping. When selecting a campsite, look for flat areas that are clear of rocks and debris. Avoid camping too close to water sources to prevent disturbing wildlife and to avoid setting up in flood-prone areas.

The Black Ridge Canyon Wilderness within the Colorado National Monument has several designated campsites, including those along the Black Ridge Loop Trail. These sites offer privacy, shelter from the wind, and a great view of the canyon walls and surrounding desert. Similarly, the Rattlesnake Arches Trail provides primitive campsites near the arches themselves, which allow you to wake up to incredible sunrise views.

For those backpacking in the McInnis Canyons, there are established backcountry campsites that are strategically located, giving hikers an opportunity to settle in before exploring the desert landscape. Ensure that you follow Leave No Trace principles and use established campsites to preserve the environment.

What to Pack:

When preparing for multi-day backpacking trips in Grand Junction, packing the right gear is essential. Start with a high-quality backpack with ample space for food, water, and extra gear. You'll need to bring a lightweight tent that's suitable for desert and mountainous environments, ensuring it's sturdy enough to withstand any wind or rain.

Don't forget a **sleeping bag** that's rated for the seasonal temperature of the region. For example, in summer, a sleeping bag rated to 30°F will suffice, but in colder months, it's important to go with a bag rated for colder temperatures. For cooking, a compact stove, lightweight cookware, and enough fuel for several days are essential.

When it comes to **food**, dehydrated meals are the go-to for most backpackers as they're lightweight and easy to prepare. Be sure to pack snacks like trail mix and energy bars to keep your energy levels up during the hike.

Always bring plenty of **water**—consider a filtering system or carry enough water for the entire trip, especially if hiking in more remote areas. A water purification system will give you access to water sources if needed along the trail.

Lastly, make sure you bring a **first aid kit**, a headlamp with extra batteries, sun protection (hat, sunscreen, sunglasses), a compass or GPS device, and an emergency whistle. These items will help ensure your safety during the adventure.

Grand Junction offers incredible multi-day hikes and backpacking routes that range from hidden gems to iconic trails with breathtaking views.

Whether you're seeking an underrated adventure, a weekend getaway, or a longer trek into the wild, these trails will offer you an unforgettable experience. Proper planning, careful packing, and an adventurous spirit will ensure that you make the most of your backpacking adventure, while leaving nothing but footprints behind.

Chapter

8

GRAND JUNCTION HIKING ITINERARIES

rand Junction is a hiker's paradise, offering everything from quick scenic hikes to multi-day backpacking adventures. Whether you have a day, a weekend, or an entire week, this region provides diverse hiking opportunities that allow you to immerse yourself in the stunning landscapes. Below are carefully crafted itineraries designed to make the most of your time in Grand Junction, helping you explore the best hikes while enjoying the local culture, food, and natural beauty.

24 Hours in Grand Junction: The Best Quick Hikes

If you're in Grand Junction for just a day, don't worry—you can still experience some of the area's best hiking spots. Here's an itinerary to help you make the most of a short stay:

Morning:

Start your day early with a visit to the Colorado National Monument, which offers some of the most iconic landscapes in the area. Begin with a quick hike on the Serpents Trail, which will take you along the **"crookedest road"** and offer stunning views of the red rock formations and distant mountain ranges. The hike is moderate, taking approximately 1 to 2 hours, perfect for a morning stretch.

Afterward, head to the Monument Canyon Trail to see the massive sandstone monoliths. This trail is short (around 2.5 miles) and relatively easy, giving you a great overview of the Monument's geology. Be sure to take your time here to capture some photos of the towering rock spires.

Lunch:

After your morning hikes, enjoy a well-deserved lunch at The Winery Restaurant in downtown Grand Junction, which offers local wines and a variety of fresh, delicious dishes. Or, if you prefer something more casual, visit Tacos Del Gordo for flavorful Mexican food.

Afternoon:

In the afternoon, explore the Riverfront Trail, a relaxing 3.5-mile hike along the Colorado River. This trail offers stunning views of the river and wildlife, and is also easily accessible if you're short on time.

To wrap up your hiking day, check out the Devil's Kitchen Trail, a short, family-friendly hike that brings you past incredible rock formations. This easy trail is perfect for winding down, as it's less than 1.5 miles and offers a tranquil end to your day.

Evening:

End your day with a relaxing dinner at Café Sol, which serves delicious organic, locally sourced meals in a cozy setting. If you have some energy left, explore downtown Grand Junction, where you can browse local shops and enjoy the charming atmosphere.

3-Day Ultimate Hiking & Sightseeing Plan (Includes Food & Rest Stop Suggestions)

For those with a little more time, a 3-day itinerary in Grand Junction will allow you to explore more of the best trails, along with local sights and experiences. Here's how to maximize your time there:

Day 1: Exploration & Scenic Views

Morning: Start your adventure at the Colorado National Monument. Begin with the Serpents Trail to get the day going with some stunning early morning views. Afterward, take a break at the Visitor Center to learn more about the history and geology of the area.

For a more challenging option, tackle the Monument Canyon Trail, which is slightly longer but offers views of massive monoliths and other geological features. Allow about 2–3 hours for this hike.

Lunch: Afterward, head to The Blue Moon Bakery for a quick lunch, offering a selection of healthy sandwiches, salads, and baked goods.

Afternoon: In the afternoon, explore the Riverfront Trail to relax and take in the peaceful river views. If you're feeling more adventurous, consider adding the Miramonte Rim Trail for some panoramic views of the area, which takes about 2–3 hours.

Dinner: Head to The Palisade Café for a local dining experience, where you can indulge in some fresh produce and locally grown dishes that capture the essence of Grand Junction.

Day 2: Discover the Desert & Natural Wonders

Morning: On your second day, visit the McInnis Canyons National Conservation Area, home to the stunning Rattlesnake Arches Trail. This challenging trail is perfect for early risers and offers fantastic views of the arches and surrounding desert. It's about 4 miles round-trip, and you'll want to take your time exploring.

Lunch: After completing your hike, head to The Goat and Clover, a farm-to-table restaurant with a variety of options, including vegetarian dishes and hearty meals.

Afternoon: In the afternoon, visit the Dinosaur Hill Trail. A family-friendly trail, this short hike (around 1.5 miles) takes you through prehistoric history, with dinosaur footprints along the way. If time allows, consider visiting the Dinosaur Journey Museum afterward for an educational experience.

Dinner: Enjoy dinner at The Silo, a cozy restaurant with outdoor seating that offers American fare with a focus on local ingredients.

Day 3: Off the Beaten Path

Morning: Start your final day with an adventure on the Serpents Trail, followed by a visit to No Thoroughfare Canyon, which features stunning hidden waterfalls and rock formations. This trail can be a bit more challenging, but the scenery makes it well worth the effort.

Lunch: Enjoy lunch at The Meltdown Grill, known for its comfort food and fantastic sandwiches.

Afternoon: Spend your afternoon at Palisade, a charming town just outside Grand Junction. Enjoy a visit to The Palisade Plunge, one of the longest downhill mountain bike trails in the country (perfect if you're looking to do something a bit different). Hike part of the trail or simply relax in the town and enjoy a wine tasting at one of the local wineries.

Dinner: End your trip with dinner at The Wine Country Inn in Palisade, offering a fine-dining experience with great views over the vineyards.

One Week in Grand Junction: A Hiker's Dream Schedule

For those who have an entire week to spend in Grand Junction, this itinerary will allow you to take a deep dive into the area's stunning landscapes, fascinating history, and outdoor adventures.

Day 1: Colorado National Monument

Begin your trip with a visit to Colorado National Monument to get your bearings. Hike the Serpents Trail and Monument Canyon Trail. In the afternoon, explore other nearby areas, such as the Devil's Kitchen or Miramonte Rim.

Day 2: McInnis Canyons National Conservation Area

Explore the Rattlesnake Arches Trail and No Thoroughfare Canyon. These stunning trails offer plenty of adventure, from rock formations to hidden waterfalls.

Day 3: Fruita's Paleo Area & Riverfront Trail

Spend the day exploring the Fruita Paleo Area and hiking the Riverfront Trail for an easy day of hiking, perfect for soaking in the Colorado River scenery. Explore local museums for insights into the region's prehistoric past.

Day 4: Hidden Gems & Wilderness

Hike to the Little Book Cliffs or visit the Black Ridge Canyon Wilderness for a more secluded, off-the-beaten-path experience. Spend the night camping in the backcountry for a true wilderness experience.

Day 5: Rest Day + Downtown Exploration

Spend a relaxing day exploring downtown Grand Junction. Visit local shops, art galleries, and have lunch at one of the farm-to-table restaurants. Consider a wine tour to experience the area's vineyards.

Day 6: Multi-Day Adventure

Tackle a longer, more challenging trail such as Rattlesnake Arches, or enjoy the full Black Ridge Loop or Grand Mesa trails.

Day 7: Palisade & Outdoor Activities

Spend your final day in Palisade, enjoying a hike, mountain biking, or relaxing in the vineyards. Consider an evening hike to the Palisade Plunge, followed by a farewell dinner at The Silo in Palisade.

Whether you're on a short day trip or an extended stay, Grand Junction offers endless opportunities for exploration. From family-friendly hikes to challenging adventures and multi-day treks, this region has something for every type of hiker. This variety ensures that no matter how much time you have, you'll experience some of the most stunning and diverse landscapes in Colorado. Happy hiking!

Chapter

9

SEASONAL HIKING IN GRAND JUNCTION

Grand Junction is a region that comes alive with the changing seasons, each one offering its own unique hiking experiences. From wildflower-filled landscapes in the spring to the summer heat and everything in between, understanding what to expect from each season will help you plan the perfect hiking trip. Below is a breakdown of the best hiking experiences during each season in Grand Junction, along with practical tips for making the most of your adventure.

Spring: Best Wildflower Trails & Waterfall Hikes

Spring in Grand Junction is a magical time of year, especially for hikers. As the snow melts, the desert landscape transforms into a colorful paradise with a burst of wildflowers and rushing waterfalls. The temperatures are moderate, making it an ideal season for outdoor exploration. Here are some of the best spring hiking experiences you can enjoy:

1. Wildflower Trails

Grand Junction's high desert and **canyonlands** are home to a vibrant display of wildflowers, making spring a prime time for hiking. The high elevation of the Colorado National Monument, along with its secluded canyons, offers a rich variety of wildflowers, including Indian paintbrush, lupine, columbine, and desert primrose. Here are a few trails where you can enjoy the blooming beauty:

Serpents Trail: This trail in the Colorado National Monument offers sweeping views of the desert landscape, with wildflowers blanketing the ground in the spring.

The colors contrast beautifully with the red rock cliffs and green juniper trees. The moderate difficulty makes it accessible for most hikers, and the 2.5-mile distance ensures you can enjoy the wildflower scenery without an all-day commitment.

No Thoroughfare Canyon: This canyon is known for its waterfalls, but in the spring, it becomes an explosion of colors. The wildflowers bloom in the grassy meadows, making this trail one of the best for spring hiking. It's a moderate hike (about 5 miles), but the diversity of flora and the sound of rushing water from the falls make it incredibly scenic.

2. Waterfall Hikes

As the snow melts from the mountain peaks, streams and waterfalls in Grand Junction come alive. Spring is the best time to experience these refreshing and breathtaking waterfalls. Here are a few popular waterfall hikes in the region:

No Thoroughfare Canyon: Known for its waterfalls, this trail features stunning rock formations and cool pools of water that are most impressive in the spring. This hike is moderate in difficulty, with a beautiful combination of waterfalls and wildflower meadows.

Mica Mine Trail: This trail is short and easy, taking you through a mining area that is dotted with glittering rocks. During the spring, this trail is a great choice if you want to enjoy some of the region's small waterfalls and the wildflowers that line the route. You'll also get a glimpse into Grand Junction's fascinating mining history.

3. Hiking Tips for Spring:

Start early in the day to avoid the heat of mid-afternoon.

Pack extra water since some areas can still be dry, despite the melting snow.

Wear sun protection, even in the spring, as the sun's reflection off of rocks and canyons can be intense.

Check trail conditions before heading out, as spring rains can sometimes make trails muddy or cause temporary closures.

Summer: Beating the Heat & Staying Hydrated on the Trail

Summer in Grand Junction can be intense, with temperatures often rising well into the 90s and even over 100°F on the hottest days. But don't let the heat discourage you—summer offers its own set of challenges and rewards for hikers. The key to enjoying summer hiking in Grand Junction is understanding how to beat the heat, stay hydrated, and plan your hikes accordingly.

1. Early Morning & Evening Hikes

The summer heat in Grand Junction is best avoided by hiking during the cooler parts of the day—early mornings or evenings. Most trails in the area are best enjoyed at sunrise or sunset when temperatures are more moderate, and the scenery is breathtaking in the golden light.

Serpents Trail: For an early morning hike, the Serpents Trail in the Colorado National Monument is a great option. The sun rises over the desert, casting long shadows and highlighting the monolithic rock formations that are iconic to the region.

It's an ideal time to catch a cool breeze and experience the desert in its most serene state.

Riverfront Trail: If you prefer a gentler hike, the Riverfront Trail is perfect for an evening stroll. This trail follows the Colorado River, offering great opportunities to spot wildlife and enjoy cooler temperatures as the sun sets.

2. Beating the Heat: Stay Cool & Hydrated

In the summer, staying hydrated is paramount. The desert landscape can be unforgiving, especially if you're hiking in the afternoon when temperatures soar. The following advice will help you stay safe in the heat:

Hydrate well before the hike: Start your hike with a full water bottle and carry at least 3 liters of water for longer hikes.

Wear light, breathable clothing: Choose clothing made of moisture-wicking fabrics, which help keep sweat off your skin and allow you to cool off.

Take breaks in shaded areas whenever possible, especially if you're feeling the heat. Many trails offer spots where you can stop and rest in the shade of trees or rock outcroppings.

Know your limits: If the temperature is extremely hot, it's best to shorten your hike or opt for a cooler trail along the river or in the higher elevations.

3. Popular Summer Trails:

In the summer, it's best to focus on trails that offer some elevation for cooler temperatures and scenic landscapes to keep your interest piqued.

Monument Canyon Trail: The Monument Canyon area in Colorado National Monument provides some cooler, shady spots under the towering rock formations. The hike is fairly moderate, and you'll have the chance to explore some of the most iconic landscapes in the area.

Palisade Plunge Trail: If you're looking for an exciting, challenging trail during summer, the Palisade Plunge is a must-do for experienced hikers. The trail starts in the highlands and descends through the canyon, offering a cooler temperature and great views throughout the hike.

4. Summer Hiking Tips:

- Start early or late to avoid the peak heat of midday.
- Carry enough water for the entire hike.
- Wear hats, sunglasses, and sunblock to protect yourself from the harsh sun.
- Opt for shaded trails or those near water to stay cool.

Each season in Grand Junction offers a unique hiking experience. Whether you're drawn to the wildflower meadows of spring or the early morning adventures of summer, this region has something for every type of hiker. By planning accordingly and taking precautions, you'll ensure a safe and enjoyable hiking experience no matter when you visit. Spring and summer in Grand Junction offer some of the most picturesque hikes, so lace up your boots and prepare for a journey that you'll never forget.

Fall: Best Trails for Colorful Foliage & Cooler Temperatures

As the summer heat subsides and cooler temperatures sweep across the Grand Junction region, fall emerges as one of the most stunning times to hike. The crisp air and colorful foliage transform the landscape, offering hikers an opportunity to experience the desert and canyonlands in an entirely new light. The golden aspen leaves, fiery red sumac, and amber-colored oaks make fall hiking a photographer's paradise. Plus, with cooler temperatures, it's an ideal season for tackling more challenging hikes without the oppressive heat of summer.

1. Best Fall Hiking Trails:

Fall hiking in Grand Junction is all about embracing the season's beauty while enjoying pleasant temperatures for outdoor exploration. Here are some trails where you can enjoy the best of fall:

Colorado National Monument: This area is a prime destination for fall foliage. As the tall aspens and maples change colors, the red rock cliffs contrast beautifully with the vibrant hues of autumn. Trails such as Monument Canyon and Serpents Trail offer views that make the hike worth every step, with cool temperatures making the journey more enjoyable. These trails are moderate, with the canyon views providing a perfect backdrop for autumn's colors.

Loma Trail System: For a variety of fall colors and the opportunity to see distant views of the Grand Mesa, the Loma Trail System is a great choice. As you hike through the canyons, the maple trees provide a warm, golden glow, while the cool breeze is a welcome relief from the summer sun.

Palisade Plunge Trail: Fall is a great time to tackle the Palisade Plunge, especially as the leaves on the high-altitude forests turn vibrant shades of yellow and red. The descent through the canyon gives you panoramic views of the valley, and the cooler weather makes the long-distance trail more manageable.

2. Fall Hiking Tips:

Layer your clothing: Fall weather can be unpredictable, with cool mornings and warmer afternoons. Wear breathable, moisture-wicking fabrics to adjust to temperature changes.

Watch for slippery conditions: As leaves fall, trails can get slippery. Take extra caution when navigating rockier paths.

Bring a camera: Fall's spectacular colors make it a prime time for photography. Don't forget to capture the landscapes at their most vibrant.

Enjoy early hikes: Sunrise hikes in fall provide a calm atmosphere with cool temperatures and the added bonus of seeing the leaves glow in the morning light.

Winter: Snowy Trails, Ice Hiking & Cold-Weather Safety Tips

Winter in Grand Junction may not bring the same intensity of snow as the higher Rocky Mountain areas, but it certainly brings an entirely different hiking experience. The desert landscape transforms into a winter wonderland, with dustings of snow covering the red rock canyons and rock formations. While it's possible to hike year-round, winter hiking in Grand Junction comes with its own set of challenges and rewards, including ice hiking and the opportunity to experience a serene, snow-covered landscape without the crowds.

1. Best Winter Hiking Trails:

Winter hiking in Grand Junction is a quieter, more peaceful experience, with trails often much less crowded than in the warmer months. Here are some of the best trails to enjoy during the winter months:

Colorado National Monument: When snow dusts the red sandstone cliffs and the canyon floors, the Colorado National Monument becomes a winter paradise. Trails such as Monument Canyon Trail and Serpents Trail provide panoramic views, with a dusting of snow creating an ethereal quality to the landscape. Even though temperatures can drop significantly, the lower elevation trails are still accessible for most hikers.

Dinosaur Hill Trail: A great trail to explore during winter, Dinosaur Hill gives hikers a glimpse into the prehistoric past. The snow-capped mountains in the background, coupled with desert terrain, make this an ideal hike for winter enthusiasts who enjoy the mix of desert and mountain scenery. The trail is relatively easy, making it a perfect choice for a winter outing.

Rattlesnake Arches Trail: For those seeking a bit of adventure in winter, the Rattlesnake Arches Trail offers the stunning second-largest arch collection in the world. The landscape is particularly magical when dusted with snow, and the more challenging aspects of the trail are often quieter during winter months.

2. Ice Hiking & Safety in Winter:

Winter hiking comes with different risks compared to other seasons. The terrain can be slippery, and conditions can change rapidly, especially in the mornings and evenings. The following advice will help you stay safe:

Wear proper footwear: Make sure your boots have good tread for snow and ice. Consider using spikes or crampons on slippery sections.

Dress warmly: Layer your clothing with insulating materials such as fleece or down, but also pack lightweight layers that wick moisture away. Be sure to wear thermal socks and waterproof gloves.

Check trail conditions: Make sure the trail is open, and check for snow accumulation or icy patches that may require extra care.

Bring extra gear: In winter, it's essential to pack extra gloves, hats, hand warmers, and emergency supplies like a first aid kit and a headlamp for shorter daylight hours.

3. Winter Hiking Tips:

Start your hike early to maximize daylight hours.

Know your limits: Winter hiking can be challenging due to the cold and changing weather conditions. Be prepared to turn back if the conditions worsen.

Stay hydrated: Even in winter, staying hydrated is important. Dehydration can be harder to notice in cold weather, so carry enough water.

Watch for frozen water sources: Trails that cross streams or creeks may have ice patches. Exercise extra caution around these areas, as ice can be unstable.

Each season in Grand Junction offers its own set of experiences that make hiking in the region an unforgettable journey. From wildflower-laden trails in spring to snowy, serene landscapes in winter, there is no wrong time to visit. Whether you're seeking the vibrancy of fall or the peaceful solitude of winter, Grand Junction's diverse terrain ensures that every season brings something special to the hiking table. By understanding what to expect and preparing accordingly, you'll be able to experience the best of Grand Junction's trails no matter the time of year. Happy hiking!

Chapter

10

Beyond Hiking: Other Adventures In Grand Junction

While hiking is the quintessential adventure in Grand Junction, there's a wealth of other exhilarating outdoor pursuits waiting for you in this vibrant area. The region's rugged landscapes, vast canyon systems, and high desert plateaus create the perfect backdrop for a wide range of outdoor activities. Whether you're looking to climb towering rock faces, tackle heart-pounding mountain biking trails, or explore the area in new and exciting ways, Grand Junction has something to satisfy every adventurer's craving.

Best Rock Climbing & Bouldering Spots

Grand Junction and the surrounding areas are renowned for their exceptional rock climbing and bouldering opportunities. With towering cliffs, canyon walls, and slickrock formations, the region offers a variety of challenges for climbers of all skill levels. Here are some of the best rock climbing and bouldering spots in Grand Junction:

1. Colorado National Monument:

The Colorado National Monument is a mecca for rock climbers, offering everything from technical sport climbing to traditional routes. Its towering sandstone cliffs, such as Independence Monument and Kissing Couple, provide routes that range in difficulty from beginner to expert.

Independence Monument: This iconic free-standing spire is a classic among climbers. Standing at 450 feet, it requires a bit of skill and experience, but the views from the top are spectacular.

Kissing Couple: This two-pronged spire offers challenging routes for advanced climbers, with technical aspects that test your strength and skill. The spire itself is considered one of the most recognizable landmarks in the Monument.

2. Rattlesnake Canyon:

Located just outside of Grand Junction, Rattlesnake Canyon offers over 500 climbing routes on steep, jagged rock formations. The canyon is particularly well-known for its sport climbing routes, with options ranging from moderate to difficult climbs. The terrain is characterized by massive overhangs and crux moves, ideal for climbers seeking a more adventurous challenge.

The Main Wall: This vertical wall offers a range of sport climbing routes that test your endurance and technique, with the added bonus of breathtaking views of the surrounding desert.

Boulder Walls: If you prefer bouldering, Rattlesnake Canyon offers multiple boulder problems, with varying difficulty levels that will keep climbers of all abilities engaged.

3. The Bookcliffs:

The Bookcliffs range, just to the north of Grand Junction, is another world-class location for rock climbing. With multi-pitch routes and a combination of trad and sport climbing, this area is perfect for climbers looking for a remote experience surrounded by rugged landscapes.

The Bookcliffs Walls: These areas are mostly trad routes, and because of the remote nature, climbers should come prepared with all necessary gear. The climbs vary in difficulty, but they provide a true wilderness experience.

4. North Fruita Desert:

The North Fruita Desert is not only a haven for mountain bikers but also a fantastic bouldering destination. The area's slickrock and sandstone offer a variety of bouldering challenges, perfect for those looking to test their technique and strength on small, powerful moves. This is an excellent location for beginners to intermediate boulderers looking for a variety of problems across different grades.

Top Mountain Biking Trails in the Region

Grand Junction is known as the "Mountain Biking Capital of the World," thanks to its extensive network of trails that cater to riders of all levels. From technical singletrack to flowy downhill runs, the area's diverse landscape offers some of the best mountain biking trails in the country. Whether you're new to mountain biking or a seasoned pro, these trails will give you a ride you'll never forget.

1. The Lunch Loops:

Located on the south side of Grand Junction, the Lunch Loops are a trail system that caters to all levels of riders, offering everything from easy flow trails to technical downhill runs. The views over the Grand Valley and the surrounding red rock formations make this one of the most scenic biking locations in the area.

Gunny Loop: This trail offers a moderate challenge, with smooth, flowing singletrack and beautiful views of the surrounding desert. It's a favorite for both local riders and visitors, making it perfect for a mid-length ride.

Kessler's Connector: For more experienced riders, Kessler's Connector provides a technical challenge, with steep climbs, descents, and challenging rock gardens. The trail connects to other Lunch Loops routes, allowing you to customize your ride.

2. Kokopelli Trails:

The Kokopelli Trails are some of the most famous mountain biking trails in the area, offering both technical terrain and long-distance routes. The trails extend for miles through the Redlands area, and the views of the Colorado River are absolutely stunning.

Mary's Loop: This trail provides a great introduction to Kokopelli Trails and features a moderate challenge. Riders enjoy flowy sections, coupled with rocky technical sections, all while enjoying spectacular views of the river below.

West Rim Trail: For more experienced riders, the West Rim Trail provides more difficult terrain with technical climbing and descending. This trail is perfect for those looking to test their skills on challenging singletrack.

3. North Fruita Desert Trails:

The North Fruita Desert is a mountain biking haven. Known for its wide variety of trails, it offers everything from beginner-friendly rides to advanced technical challenges. The area's slickrock and wide open spaces make it one of the best spots for desert mountain biking.

The 18 Road Trails: These are some of the best beginner and intermediate trails in the region. The flowy loops and easy climbs allow riders to focus on developing skills while enjoying the beauty of the desert.

Joe's Ridge: For intermediate to advanced riders, Joe's Ridge offers rocky ascents, technical descents, and thrilling downhill sections. The trail has a variety of terrain that keeps things interesting, and riders can take in expansive views of the desert as they navigate the trail.

4. Palisade Plunge:

A bucket-list trail for serious mountain bikers, the Palisade Plunge is a 26-mile trail that offers a descent of over 4,000 feet from the top of the Grand Mesa to the valley floor below. The trail includes everything from fast, flowy sections to technical rock gardens, with amazing views of the surrounding area. The Palisade Plunge is perfect for those seeking an unforgettable downhill adventure.

Grand Junction is truly a paradise for outdoor adventurers, and its reputation extends well beyond hiking. Whether you're an aspiring rock climber looking for towering cliffs to scale or a mountain biking enthusiast eager to tackle world-class trails, Grand Junction has it all. From rocky canyons to slickrock formations, the region offers outdoor pursuits for every type of adventurer. So, lace up your climbing shoes or hop on your mountain bike and get ready to experience Grand Junction in ways you never imagined!

Rafting & Kayaking on the Colorado River

One of the most exhilarating ways to experience the natural beauty of Grand Junction and its surrounding landscapes is through rafting and kayaking on the mighty Colorado River. This winding waterway is not only a crucial part of the region's ecosystem but also an adventure lover's playground. Whether you're a seasoned kayaker or a first-time rafter, the Colorado River offers an array of thrilling water experiences in the heart of the desert.

1. Colorado River Rafting – An Adventure for All Levels

Rafting on the Colorado River is an adventure that provides unique views of the region's striking red rock cliffs, desert landscapes, and wildlife. There are several companies in Grand Junction offering guided rafting trips, and the rapids range from mild to moderate, making it ideal for families, beginner paddlers, and those seeking a more relaxing yet scenic journey.

Ruby-Horsethief Canyon: This remote, pristine stretch of the Colorado River offers a laid-back rafting experience. You'll float through wild canyons, with occasional rapids that provide just enough thrill for first-timers and families. Along the way, take in views of towering cliffs and wildlife, such as bald eagles, bighorn sheep, and the occasional river otter.

Westwater Canyon: For those with a bit more rafting experience, Westwater Canyon offers Class III-IV rapids, perfect for those seeking a more intense rafting adventure.

Known for its dramatic black rock walls and rugged terrain, this stretch of the river is both thrilling and awe-inspiring, offering adrenaline-pumping rapids alongside serene moments of relaxation.

2. Kayaking for a More Intimate River Experience

If you're looking to get closer to the water and enjoy a more personal connection with the river, kayaking on the Colorado is a great option. Kayakers can explore the quieter parts of the river, where the waters are still and serene, allowing for peaceful paddles through desert landscapes and lush riparian areas.

Flatwater Kayaking: If you're looking for a less intense experience, flatwater kayaking is perfect for a relaxing paddle along the Colorado River. Explore scenic sections such as Ruby-Horsethief Canyon, where the river meanders through breathtaking landscapes, offering views of lush wetlands and wildlife.

Fishing & Kayaking Combo: For fishing enthusiasts, kayaking can be combined with some catch-and-release fishing in the Colorado River. The waterway is home to various fish species, including trout, smallmouth bass, and walleye. Paddle along the river and try your hand at fishing in a peaceful, quiet environment.

Where to Go for the Best Sunset Views (Popular Among Photographers & Casual Explorers)

Grand Junction is known for its stunning sunsets, with the desert landscapes and red rock formations creating a perfect backdrop for breathtaking displays of color. Whether you're a photographer or just someone who enjoys a peaceful end to your day, there are several spots around Grand Junction that offer some of the best sunset views in the region.

1. Colorado National Monument

One of the most iconic places to watch the sunset is the Colorado National Monument. With its towering sandstone monoliths, deep canyons, and expansive views, the park is a photographer's dream during the golden hour. The Western Rim Road and Visitor Center Overlook are two of the most popular spots to catch the sunset.

The Fruita Canyon Overlook: This spot provides a stunning panoramic view of the valley and the red rock cliffs as the sun dips below the horizon, casting vibrant hues of pink, orange, and purple across the sky. It's a popular location for photographers and casual explorers alike, and the park's remote feel gives it a peaceful atmosphere as the day comes to a close.

2. Monument Peak

For those willing to take a moderate hike, Monument Peak offers a fantastic sunset view. The peak provides a unique perspective of the Colorado National Monument and the Grand Valley, offering a sweeping 360-degree view. As the sun sets, the entire valley is bathed in a warm, golden glow, perfect for snapping a few memorable shots.

3. Lunch Loops

If you're looking for a quick and easy way to enjoy a great sunset, the Lunch Loops area is another top pick. A favorite spot among locals and photographers, the West Rim Trail offers an incredible sunset view overlooking the Grand Valley. The rugged terrain and rolling hills surrounding the area create a dramatic backdrop, with red rock cliffs casting long shadows as the sun sets.

Best Local Breweries & Wineries for a Post-Hike Drink

After a long day on the trails or a thrilling river adventure, there's nothing better than relaxing with a refreshing drink at one of Grand Junction's local breweries or wineries. The region has a growing reputation for its craft beer scene and award-winning wineries, offering the perfect place to unwind and soak in the local atmosphere.

1. Kannah Creek Brewing Company

For beer enthusiasts, Kannah Creek Brewing Company is a must-visit. Known for its wide selection of craft beers, this local brewery offers everything from IPAs to dark stouts. The laid-back vibe makes it a great spot to hang out with fellow hikers, share stories of your adventures, and enjoy a freshly poured pint. The Riverfront IPA is a favorite, and the brewery's outdoor patio provides scenic views, making it the perfect place to unwind after a hike.

2. Western Colorado's Wine Country

Grand Junction is part of Colorado's Wine Country, and you'll find a number of local wineries offering exquisite wines and great food. Visit Talon Winery for some of the best local wines, where you can sample everything from chardonnay to merlot, all produced right on the estate. The winery offers a relaxing atmosphere where you can sit on the patio, enjoy a glass of wine, and watch the sunset over the surrounding vineyards.

3. Spero Winery

Another local gem is Spero Winery, known for its small-batch, hand-crafted wines. With a wide variety of reds, whites, and blends, this winery creates a perfect post-hike destination. The winery's tasting room is cozy, and the scenic outdoor area lets you enjoy your drink while soaking up the stunning Mesa views. Spero's Cabernet Franc and Sauvignon Blanc are fan favorites and perfect companions after a day of hiking or kayaking.

4. Edgewater Brewing Company

For a relaxed, riverside atmosphere, head over to Edgewater Brewing Company. Located right by the Colorado River, the brewery offers a variety of craft beers and delicious bites. Whether you're in the mood for a refreshing pale ale or a hearty lager, Edgewater is the perfect place to relax after an adventure-filled day. The brewery's proximity to the river means you can enjoy great views while sipping on a drink.

Grand Junction is not just a destination for hiking and mountain biking—it's a place that offers a wide array of outdoor adventures. From the thrill of rafting and kayaking the Colorado River to the beauty of sunset views and local breweries, the region provides something for everyone. Whether you're seeking a relaxing day on the river or looking to enjoy a post-adventure drink at a local winery or brewery, Grand Junction ensures your adventure doesn't end when the hike does.

Chapter

11

Local Insights & Expert Tips

One of the best ways to enhance your hiking experience in Grand Junction is by tapping into the knowledge of local experts. From seasoned hikers to park rangers who know the land like the back of their hand, the insight they provide can help you not only stay safe but also discover hidden gems off the beaten path. This section is dedicated to offering you local insights and expert tips that will make your time in Grand Junction not only safer but more enriching.

Interviews with Local Hikers & Park Rangers

Local hikers and park rangers are invaluable resources when it comes to understanding the nuances of hiking in Grand Junction. They know the region's trails inside and out, from easily accessible pathways to the more challenging backcountry routes. Here's some advice straight from the experts:

Sarah Matthews – Local Hiker:

Sarah Matthews, a long-time resident of Grand Junction, shares some great advice for first-time visitors: "Grand Junction is a hidden gem, and one of the best parts of hiking here is the diversity of trails. If you're new to the area, don't underestimate the weather—temperatures can change quickly, so always pack extra layers. The Liberty Cap Trail and Echo Canyon are must-dos for those looking for moderate hikes with scenic views, but for something quieter, try the Mica Mine Trail. Less traveled, but definitely rewarding."

John Simmons – Park Ranger at Colorado National Monument:

John, a park ranger with years of experience at Colorado National Monument, highlights the importance of respecting nature. "Many people think they can hike here without any consequences, but it's vital to follow the Leave No Trace principles. We're in a fragile desert ecosystem—especially on trails like Ute Canyon and Monument Canyon. Always stay on the trail, and be mindful of wildlife. Snakes, including rattlesnakes, are common in the warmer months, so always keep an eye on your surroundings."

John also mentions a little-known spot for advanced hikers: Rattlesnake Arches Trail. "It's one of the longest, most remote trails in the region, but it offers a unique collection of arches and canyons that you can't find anywhere else in the U.S."

The History & Geology of Grand Junction's Landscapes

Grand Junction's landscapes are more than just beautiful; they're full of rich history and geological significance that stretch back millions of years. Understanding the geology and history of this area will deepen your appreciation for the trails you walk and the mountains you climb.

1. Geological Formation:

Grand Junction's geology tells a story of ancient seas, volcanic activity, and erosion. The area sits at the meeting point of the Colorado Plateau, the Great Basin, and the Rocky Mountains, resulting in an astonishing variety of landscapes, from flat desert plains to rugged mountain peaks. The Colorado National Monument is one of the most stunning examples of the region's geology, featuring towering sandstone monoliths and deep canyons that have been carved over millions of years by wind and water.

Sandstone Monoliths: The towering red rock formations in the area are the result of sedimentary deposits that accumulated in ancient rivers and lakes. Over time, tectonic forces lifted the land, and erosion exposed the vibrant sandstone cliffs and monolithic structures.

Rattlesnake Arches: The second-largest arch collection in the world, located in Rattlesnake Canyon, was formed by wind erosion, slowly eroding the rock into arches that now dot the landscape like natural sculptures.

2. Fossil Evidence:

The region is also rich in fossils that provide a glimpse into prehistoric times. Grand Junction is home to several fossil-rich sites, with the Fruita Paleo Area being a particularly notable location. Here, you'll find footprints and bone fragments from dinosaurs that once roamed the land millions of years ago. Dinosaur Hill is another spot that showcases fossil tracks, along with remnants of ancient riverbeds and forests.

3. Native American History:

Before the area became a hub for hikers and adventurers, Grand Junction was home to indigenous tribes, including the Ute people, who lived in the region for thousands of years. Evidence of their existence can still be found in the area, from petroglyphs and rock art to the remains of ancient villages. The Ute Canyon Trail is named after this tribe, and hikers can learn about the area's Native American history as they explore the route.

4. The Influence of the Colorado River:

The Colorado River has played a significant role in shaping the land, cutting through the rock over millennia to form dramatic canyons and providing essential water resources to the region's ecosystems. The river is integral to the Grand Valley, nourishing both the natural landscapes and the communities that call it home.

5. A Diverse Ecosystem:

Due to its varied terrain, Grand Junction is home to a wide range of ecosystems, from desert scrubland to riparian zones along the Colorado River. This diversity results in rich biodiversity, and hikers will likely encounter everything from cactus and sagebrush to cottonwood trees and wildflowers. Understanding the geology and history of the region will help you better appreciate the complex interactions between the land, water, and life that make Grand Junction such a special place to explore.

Expert Tips for Hiking in Grand Junction

Stay Hydrated: The desert climate can be deceiving, with intense sun during the day and cool nights. Always carry plenty of water, especially on longer hikes. A hydration pack is highly recommended.

Layer Your Clothing: Grand Junction's weather can be unpredictable. During the summer, temperatures can soar, while evenings can cool off dramatically. Dress in layers and bring a lightweight jacket for higher elevations.

Know Your Limits: Some of Grand Junction's trails are more demanding than they appear, so it's essential to know your own fitness level and experience. Start with easier trails before tackling the more challenging routes like Rattlesnake Arches or Palisade Plunge.

Wildlife Safety: While hiking, be mindful of wildlife. Rattlesnakes are common, especially in warmer months. Wear sturdy boots and be cautious around rock piles and shrubs, where snakes like to hide.

Leave No Trace: Honor the environment by abiding by the Leave No Trace philosophy. Pack out all trash, stay on marked trails, and respect wildlife from a safe distance.

Incorporating local insights and expert tips into your hike will enhance your experience, deepen your understanding of the area, and ensure that you are well-prepared for the adventure ahead. Whether you're hiking along the rugged terrain of Monument Canyon or paddling the Colorado River, these tips and historical context will guide you toward making the most of your Grand Junction hiking experience.

Chapter

12

Trail Safety: What to Do in Case of an Emergency

Hiking in Grand Junction offers breathtaking views and challenging terrain, but like any outdoor adventure, it's important to prepare for emergencies. Whether you're tackling a multi-day trek or a short family-friendly trail, understanding trail safety is crucial for ensuring your well-being and the safety of your fellow hikers. Here's what to do in case of an emergency:

1. Stay Calm and Assess the Situation

The first and most important step when facing any emergency is to remain calm. Panic can cloud your judgment and hinder your ability to think clearly. Whether you've gotten lost, encountered wildlife, or someone in your group has been injured, assessing the situation is vital.

If someone is injured, check if they are conscious and breathing.

If you're lost, try to retrace your steps to find a familiar landmark.

If you spot a dangerous animal, keep a safe distance and slowly back away.

2. Call for Help (Emergency Services)

Most of Grand Junction's popular trails are accessible, but cellular service can be spotty, especially in remote areas. If you're in a place with service, call 911 immediately to report the emergency. Be ready to provide specific details:

Location: Give as much detail about your surroundings as possible, such as trail names, landmarks, or nearby towns.

Nature of the Emergency: Whether it's an injury, lost person, or wildlife encounter, be clear about the situation.

Your Contact Information: Stay on the line if possible and follow any instructions given by the operator.

If you're in an area with no cell service, consider carrying a satellite phone or a personal locator beacon (PLB). These devices can send distress signals even in remote areas, which could save valuable time.

3. Basic First Aid

If you or someone in your group is injured, knowing basic first aid can be life-saving. Here are a few things to keep in mind:

Cuts and Scrapes: Clean the wound with water and cover it with a sterile bandage.

Sprained Ankles or Broken Bones: If someone twists an ankle or sustains a fracture, immobilize the injured area and avoid movement. If necessary, splint the injury with nearby materials (such as branches or trekking poles) until help arrives.

Heat Exhaustion/Heatstroke: On hot days, symptoms can include nausea, dizziness, and fatigue. Move to a shaded area, drink water, and cool down the body with wet cloths.

Hypothermia: In colder months, hypothermia can set in quickly. Symptoms include shivering, confusion, and slurred speech. Wrap up in warm clothing, keep moving to generate body heat, and seek shelter immediately.

4. Be Prepared for Navigation Issues

Getting lost is one of the most common concerns for hikers, especially in areas with few trail markers or in the backcountry.

Always bring a map and compass or a GPS device, even if you think you're on a well-marked trail. Here's what you can do if you find yourself lost:

Stop Moving: Avoid wandering aimlessly, as this can make it harder for rescuers to find you. Instead, find a safe place to sit and assess your surroundings.

Look for Landmarks: Try to identify key features like rivers, rock formations, or trail intersections. Use these landmarks to guide you back to a familiar path or to communicate your location to emergency responders.

Make Noise: If you're in an area where there's a chance someone will pass by, use a whistle or shout occasionally to alert others to your location.

5. Emergency Kit Essentials

A well-packed emergency kit can make all the difference in a crisis. Essential items should include:

First Aid Supplies: Bandages, antiseptic wipes, pain relievers, blister treatment, and any personal medications.

Emergency Shelter: A lightweight emergency bivy sack or space blanket to protect you from the elements.

Fire Starting Tools: Waterproof matches, a lighter, or a fire starter to provide warmth in case of an emergency.

Extra Food and Water: A few energy bars, nuts, and extra water can sustain you if you're stranded longer than anticipated.

Whistle and Mirror: For signaling rescuers if needed.

Remember that preparation is key—by knowing what to do in an emergency, you increase your chances of staying safe in unpredictable outdoor environments.

How to Avoid the Biggest Mistakes Hikers Make in Grand Junction

While hiking in Grand Junction can be an incredible experience, there are several common mistakes that hikers often make, especially when they are unfamiliar with the area or underestimate the terrain. Avoiding these pitfalls can help ensure a more enjoyable and safer hike:

1. Underestimating the Terrain

Grand Junction's trails can be deceptively challenging, especially for beginners. What might look like a short, easy trail on a map can turn out to be steep, rocky, or exposed to the sun. A common mistake hikers make is assuming a trail will be easier than it really is.

How to Avoid It: Always research a trail before hitting the trailhead. Read trail descriptions, reviews, and maps. If you're new to the area or the trail seems intimidating, start with shorter, easier hikes before tackling more challenging ones like the Palisade Plunge or Rattlesnake Arches Trail.

2. Overpacking or Underpacking

Packing the right amount of gear is crucial. Overpacking can weigh you down, making your hike more difficult, while underpacking can leave you vulnerable if unexpected situations arise.

How to Avoid It: Pack only what you need for the trail you're tackling. If you're on a short, family-friendly hike, a small daypack with water, snacks, and a first aid kit is usually enough. For longer hikes, consider additional items like extra clothing, a headlamp, or extra water.

3. Ignoring Weather Conditions

Grand Junction's weather can be unpredictable, especially in higher elevations or during transitional seasons. Failing to check the forecast can lead to exposure to extreme heat, cold weather, or unexpected storms.

How to Avoid It: Always check the weather forecast before heading out and pack accordingly. In the summer, be prepared for hot temperatures and consider hiking early in the morning or later in the evening to avoid the midday heat. In winter, pack layers and be mindful of snow conditions.

4. Not Staying on the Trail

While it's tempting to explore off-trail in such a wild, beautiful area, straying from marked paths can lead to environmental damage, make you lose your bearings, and even put you in dangerous terrain.

How to Avoid It: Always stay on marked trails. If you venture off-trail to take pictures or explore, be mindful not to damage plants, disturb wildlife, or leave a mark on the landscape. Respect the Leave No Trace principles to help preserve the beauty of Grand Junction for future generations.

5. Forgetting to Hydrate & Eat

Dehydration and hunger can strike quickly, especially in the dry desert climate of Grand Junction. Even on shorter hikes, it's easy to underestimate how much water you'll need, or to skip meals while you're focused on the trail.

How to Avoid It: Carry at least two liters of water for a half-day hike and more for longer trails. Consider packing high-energy snacks like trail mix, energy bars, or fruit to keep your energy levels up.

6. Overestimating Physical Fitness

Grand Junction offers a variety of hikes, but some trails— especially those in higher elevations or with steep inclines— require good physical fitness. Even experienced hikers may find themselves exhausted if they push beyond their limits.

How to Avoid It: Know your fitness level and choose trails that match it. If you're not used to elevation or long distances, it's better to start with an easy or moderate trail before attempting strenuous routes.

7. Not Bringing a Map or Navigation Device

Getting lost can happen quickly in unfamiliar terrain. A lack of preparation regarding navigation tools is one of the most common mistakes hikers make in Grand Junction.

How to Avoid It: Always bring a trail map, compass, or GPS device. Even if the trail is marked, it's a good idea to have a backup to avoid unnecessary confusion if trail markers are unclear or worn out.

By preparing properly, understanding the unique challenges of Grand Junction's terrain, and following expert advice, you can ensure a safe and fulfilling hiking adventure. Avoiding these common mistakes will not only enhance your experience but also help you make the most of everything this stunning destination has to offer.

Chapter

13

Practical Resources & Final Thoughts

As you embark on your hiking adventure in Grand Junction, it's important to be well-equipped with the right resources to make your trip safer, easier, and more enjoyable. Whether you're looking for navigation tools, places to rent hiking gear, or emergency contacts, this section covers all the essentials that will help ensure your hike is a success.

Best Hiking Apps & GPS Tools for Navigating Grand Junction

Navigating the diverse and rugged terrain of Grand Junction requires up-to-date, reliable tools. While paper maps and trail signs are helpful, the right technology can make your hiking experience more efficient and safer. Here are some of the top hiking apps and GPS tools for the area:

AllTrails: One of the most popular apps for hikers, AllTrails offers detailed trail maps, user reviews, and photos. You can filter trails by difficulty, length, and popularity, making it easy to find the perfect hike. The app also allows you to download maps for offline use, which is crucial in areas where cell service can be spotty.

Gaia GPS: If you're looking for a more advanced GPS tool, Gaia GPS offers topographic maps, satellite imagery, and offline navigation. This app is ideal for backcountry explorers and those venturing on multi-day backpacking trips. It's especially helpful for understanding elevation changes, finding water sources, and staying on track.

Komoot: Known for its detailed planning features, Komoot lets you customize routes for hiking, biking, and even trail running.

It provides step-by-step navigation and integrates seamlessly with your smartphone's GPS, helping you stay on the right path even in remote areas.

Maps.me: For hikers seeking offline functionality, Maps.me is an excellent free option. It offers detailed, downloadable maps and is especially useful in areas where you might not have internet access. While not specifically focused on hiking, it's still a handy tool for navigating trails and points of interest in Grand Junction.

Having one or more of these apps on hand will ensure you don't get lost or miss out on key landmarks. Just remember to bring a portable power bank to keep your devices charged throughout the day!

Where to Rent or Buy Hiking Gear Locally

If you've traveled to Grand Junction and realized you've left some crucial hiking gear behind, or if you need to upgrade your equipment, there are several local stores and outfitters where you can rent or purchase hiking gear.

Mesa Outdoor: A locally-owned store that offers a wide range of outdoor gear, including hiking shoes, backpacks, and camping equipment. They have knowledgeable staff who can help you choose the right gear for your needs.

Canyon View Sports: Specializing in outdoor and adventure gear, Canyon View Sports provides everything from hiking boots to climbing equipment. They also offer rentals for camping gear and bikes, which could be useful if you're planning on exploring Grand Junction's diverse trails.

REI (Grand Junction): For those looking for high-quality, durable hiking gear, REI's Grand Junction location offers an extensive range of outdoor products. From tents to GPS devices, they stock everything you need for a day hike or multi-day adventure. They also offer gear rentals for more specific needs, such as tents and sleeping bags for backpackers.

Sportsman's Warehouse: Another great spot for purchasing hiking gear in Grand Junction, Sportsman's Warehouse offers everything from trekking poles to hydration packs. The store's knowledgeable staff can help guide your gear choices.

It's worth checking out local rental options if you're only in town for a short time or if you don't want to haul a lot of heavy equipment with you.

Emergency Contacts & First Aid Advice for Hikers

Hiking in Grand Junction, especially on more remote trails, means you should always be prepared for emergencies. Familiarize yourself with important contacts and know what to do if an emergency arises.

Emergency Contacts:

911: For all emergencies, dial 911. If you're in an area with limited cell service, try to find high ground or a clear line of sight to improve reception.

Mesa County Sheriff's Department: For non-emergency situations or if you're lost and need assistance, call the sheriff's department at (970) 244-3500. They can provide guidance or direct you to local ranger assistance.

Bureau of Land Management (BLM) Grand Junction Office: The BLM manages a significant amount of the public land in the area. You can reach them at (970) 244-3000 for questions about trail closures, permits, or wilderness area regulations.

First Aid Advice:

Basic First Aid: Be familiar with basic first aid techniques like bandaging wounds, splinting injuries, and treating blisters. Make sure your first aid kit includes supplies for burns, cuts, insect stings, and bites.

Dehydration & Heat Stroke: The desert climate can cause dehydration quickly. Drink plenty of water, especially on longer hikes, and be aware of the symptoms of heat stroke, such as dizziness, nausea, and confusion. If you or someone in your group shows these symptoms, get to a shaded area, hydrate, and rest.

Hypothermia: On colder or higher-altitude trails, especially during the fall and winter months, be cautious of hypothermia. Signs include shivering, confusion, and slurred speech. If you notice these symptoms, add layers of clothing, take shelter, and seek immediate medical help.

Always carry a whistle, mirror, or other signaling device to alert rescuers if needed.

Final Thoughts: Making the Most of Your Grand Junction Hiking Experience

Grand Junction is a hiker's paradise, offering a variety of trails that cater to all skill levels, from easy scenic hikes to challenging multi-day treks. The region's unique combination of red rock landscapes, towering monoliths, and vast desert vistas provide an unforgettable outdoor experience.

To truly make the most of your Grand Junction hiking experience, remember that preparation is key. Be sure to research your trails ahead of time, pack appropriately, and always respect nature by following Leave No Trace principles. Whether you're embarking on a short family-friendly hike or tackling a multi-day backcountry adventure, Grand Junction's trails offer a variety of rewards.

Above all, don't rush the journey. Take time to soak in the incredible landscapes, appreciate the diversity of flora and fauna, and enjoy the sense of adventure that comes with exploring new trails. The local hiking community is warm and welcoming, and the memories you create here will last long after you've returned home.

Grand Junction is a place that invites you to discover the outdoors, challenge yourself, and leave with a greater appreciation for nature. Whether you're an experienced hiker or a beginner, there's a perfect trail waiting for you—get out there and make the most of every step. Happy hiking!

Chapter

14

Conclusion

Grand Junction is an exceptional destination for hikers of all levels, offering a diverse range of trails set against a backdrop of stunning desert landscapes, towering red rock formations, and expansive canyons. Whether you're looking for an easy family-friendly walk along the Colorado River or a challenging multi-day trek through rugged wilderness, Grand Junction has something to suit every adventure seeker. The variety of terrain, combined with the region's fascinating history and geology, ensures that each hike is more than just an outdoor activity—it's an immersive experience.

Throughout this guide, we've explored everything you need to know to plan the perfect hiking adventure, from the best trails by difficulty and season to the essential gear you'll need to stay safe on the trails. We've highlighted local insights, expert tips, and practical resources to help you navigate the trails with confidence. Grand Junction is a place where you can connect with nature, push your physical limits, and create memories that will last a lifetime.

As you venture into these landscapes, remember that hiking responsibly is crucial—respect the environment, follow Leave No Trace principles, and always be prepared. Your safety and enjoyment depend on being well-equipped and informed.

Ultimately, Grand Junction is a hiker's dream, offering unforgettable experiences that will leave you longing to return again and again. Whether you're here for a day, a weekend, or longer, your adventure in Grand Junction will be an experience worth savoring. So lace up your boots, grab your pack, and set out to explore one of Colorado's most captivating hiking destinations. Happy trails!

Chapter

15

Bonus Section: Frequently Asked Questions (FAQ)

1. **What is the best time of year to hike in Grand Junction**? The best time to hike in Grand Junction is during the spring and fall months (April to June and September to November). During these seasons, the weather is milder, and the trails are less crowded, offering a more enjoyable hiking experience. Summer can get quite hot, especially in the desert areas, and winter hiking can be challenging due to snow and freezing temperatures. However, each season offers unique beauty and experiences, so choose based on your preferences and the type of hike you're planning.

2. **Are the trails in Grand Junction suitable for beginners**? Yes! Grand Junction has a variety of beginner-friendly trails, such as the Riverfront Trail and Dinosaur Hill Trail, which are easy to navigate and perfect for families or those just starting their hiking adventures. For those looking for a bit more of a challenge, there are also moderate trails that offer a balance of stunning views and manageable difficulty.

3. **Do I need permits for hiking in Grand Junction**? Most of the popular hiking trails in Grand Junction do not require permits, but some areas—such as backcountry or multi-day hikes—may require a permit. Always check with local authorities or the Bureau of Land Management (BLM) for up-to-date information on permits, especially if you plan to camp or hike in more remote areas.

4. **What should I bring on my hike in Grand Junction**? Packing smart is key to a safe and enjoyable hike. Essentials include plenty of water (especially in warmer months), sunscreen, sturdy hiking boots, a first aid kit, a hat, and snacks. Depending on the length and difficulty of the trail, you may also need a map or GPS device, rain gear, and a headlamp for evening hikes.

5. **Are there any guided tours available in Grand Junction**? Yes, there are several local tour companies that offer guided hikes, providing expert knowledge about the region's geology, history, and wildlife. A guided tour can be an excellent option for those new to hiking or who want to learn more about the area.

New Updates & Expectations in 2025

As hiking in Grand Junction continues to grow in popularity, 2025 brings a host of exciting updates and developments for hikers. Here's what to expect:

1. **Trail Improvements & New Trail Openings**: Expect several trail enhancements in 2025, including improved signage, trail maintenance, and some new routes that offer even more diversity in the types of hiking experiences available. The Bureau of Land Management (BLM) and local organizations are continually working on preserving and enhancing the trail network, ensuring sustainability and accessibility for hikers of all levels.

2. **Eco-Friendly Initiatives**: In response to growing environmental concerns, there will be a stronger focus on Leave No Trace principles and eco-friendly hiking practices. Expect more educational programs at trailheads, as well as efforts to reduce human impact on local ecosystems. Additionally, more trails may feature waste disposal stations and designated areas for wildlife observation.

3. **Expanding Outdoor Adventure Offerings**: In 2025, Grand Junction will see an expansion in its outdoor adventure offerings. This includes increased opportunities for rock climbing, kayaking, and mountain biking, as well as enhanced access to guided tours and adventure packages.

These activities will complement the hiking experience, allowing visitors to fully explore the region's rugged beauty.

4. **Digital Enhancements for Hikers**: With the rise of smartphone technology, new digital resources for hikers will be introduced. Expect more interactive trail apps with real-time trail conditions, weather updates, and GPS-guided hiking features. These apps will provide hikers with better tools to plan their adventures and ensure they are prepared for any changes in weather or trail conditions.

5. **Sustainable Travel Initiatives**: Grand Junction's tourism industry is expected to continue shifting toward more sustainable and responsible tourism practices in 2025. This includes more emphasis on local businesses that promote eco-tourism, sustainable hiking gear rentals, and efforts to reduce carbon footprints while hiking. Expect more opportunities to explore local culture, support small businesses, and contribute to the preservation of the area's natural beauty.

With these exciting updates, 2025 promises to be an incredible year for hiking in Grand Junction. Whether you're a seasoned hiker or a first-time adventurer, the region's trails and outdoor activities will continue to provide unforgettable experiences in the coming year and beyond.

Made in the USA
Monee, IL
30 April 2025

16646185R00079